TRENDBOOK
2021-2022

National Association
of Independent Schools

ISBN: 978-1-63115-047-0
Printed in the United States of America

National Association
of Independent Schools

The National Association of Independent Schools provides services to
more than 1,900 schools and associations of schools in the United States
and abroad, including more than 1,600 nonprofit, private K-12 schools in
the U.S. that are self-determining in mission and program and are governed
by independent boards. As the largest association of independent schools,
NAIS co-creates the future of education by uniting and empowering
our community.

For more information, go to the NAIS website at
http://www.nais.org.

Editors: Susan Hunt, Myra McGovern, Karla Taylor
Design: Fletcher Design, Inc./Washington, DC
Photographers: James Kegley Photography; Anne-Marie Balzano photo by Sabrina
Harless Photography; Margaret Anne Rowe photo by Fazio Photography; Jackie
Wolking photo by Inspire Photography

TABLE OF CONTENTS

EXECUTIVE SUMMARY

By Myra McGovern and Karla Taylor

I t was a year like none we've ever experienced—and like none we ever want to experience again. During the worldwide COVID-19 pandemic, all of society has struggled with unprecedented difficulties, and independent schools have not been spared. Fortunately, the vast majority have been able to rise to the challenges of teaching online, operating safely, and creating community virtually.

The extraordinary conditions of 2020-2021 occurred against the backdrop of long-term trends that NAIS and other organizations have tracked for decades. These include not only falling birthrates and rising affordability issues but also positive changes, such as record numbers of women and people of color becoming heads of school.

But of course, some trends were new and shifted rapidly. To keep these in perspective, in April 2020 NAIS introduced in-the-moment member polls. As of June 2021, 50 Snapshot Surveys had offered insights into the impact of the coronavirus and the governmental, economic, and social responses. Snapshot Survey results appear in several of the *2021-2022 Trendbook*'s chapters. The goal is to provide the most current information available on everything from enrollment and advancement to workforce issues and student well-being.

To help your school keep up with the context in which it must operate, this edition of the *Trendbook*—the 12th—summarizes 30 important trends. All are based on in-depth research and examined from the unique independent school perspective. At the end of each of the 10 chapters are Strategic Questions designed to prompt discussion among your school leaders, board, staff, and faculty. Action Steps and Resources suggest future directions and offer guideposts to find more information.

Here's an overview of the trends in this volume.

The Economic Outlook

- After peaking during the early months of the pandemic in 2020, the unemployment rate declined rapidly. But it remains higher for some groups as of summer 2021.
- Economic growth rebounded quickly after the initial COVID shutdown. However, almost half of workers reported a loss of income between March 2020 and April 2021.
- Although some obstacles remain, economists and consumers are optimistic that jobs and economic output will continue to recover through calendar year 2021.

The Demographic Outlook

- Population growth has slowed over the past decade, a trend that may have been worsened by the pandemic.
- Diversification in the United States continues to be driven by the young.
- The pandemic has caused many people—especially young adults—to move around the United States.

The Enrollment Outlook

- Median enrollment declined in response to the pandemic.
- Enrollment has varied by school type, with lower schools and lower divisions struggling more than upper schools, and smaller schools struggling more than larger ones.
- Early indicators suggest increased applications and acceptances in 2021-2022.

The Affordability and Demand Outlook

- The pandemic worsened challenges to access and affordability, but most schools did not reduce tuition.
- Instead of adjusting tuition, many schools offered more financial aid.
- For many families, especially those with young children, switching to a different type of school was common during the pandemic.

The Philanthropy Outlook

- The pandemic did not damage annual fund and capital campaign giving for most schools.
- Online fundraising, giving via mobile devices, and virtual events all increased.
- 2020-2021 presented a "giving moment" when more donors gave, which may present nonprofits—including schools—with the opportunity to expand the future pool of supporters.

The Governance and Leadership Outlook

- Heads gave their boards positive marks during the pandemic's first year and largely found the leadership partnership to be good.
- The crisis amplified the stress that school heads feel even in normal times.
- Despite the pandemic, the overall rate of head of school job transitions remained flat. But more turnover is likely in the future.

The Workforce Outlook

- The makeup of the workforce is shifting and will affect schools as well as other sectors.
- The shift to remote work will have both positive and negative effects on institutional culture, retention, and productivity.
- A greater focus on engagement, well-being, and collaboration will drive both the types of jobs that post-pandemic workers take and the length of time they stay in their jobs.

The Equity and Justice Outlook

- A record number of women and people of color have become heads of school, although these groups are still underrepresented.
- Salary gaps by gender persist.
- Many independent schools have acted in support of diversity, equity, and inclusion, but in some areas of education, conflicts have surfaced regarding anti-racism activities and Critical Race Theory (CRT).

The Well-Being Outlook

- Although independent school students remain highly engaged in academics, teachers note that their students suffer from concerns ranging from anxiety to family health worries. Research also shows a downward trend in resilience-related skills.
- Teacher support is crucial to students, but this has implications for teacher burnout and retention.
- As schools work to mitigate learning loss, they also need to prioritize student well-being.

The Learning and Teaching Outlook

- Even as schools return to in-person learning, they continue to be open to virtual options in certain situations.
- The focus on social-emotional learning will likely continue in the future.
- Some schools are likely to keep conducting professional development virtually.

Whether your school is grappling with short-term changes or long-term challenges, the *Trendbook* is only one of the many ways NAIS can help. Take advantage of the wealth of resources available to all member schools at www.nais.org. Analyze your school's trends in the context of your market through NAIS's online statistical center, Data and Analysis for School Leadership (DASL), and the Market View tool.

And as long as pandemic conditions persist, watch for updates to NAIS's online repository of COVID-19 resources. These include legal advisories, survey templates, decision-making toolkits, forecasting guides, and wellness information.

In the epilogue to the *2021-2022 Trendbook*, NAIS President Donna Orem writes, "If there's one thing we've learned from the COVID-19 pandemic, it is that we can't predict the future. However, we *can* plan for potential impacts to our school communities." As you think ahead to the impact of future trends on your school, please share your comments and questions with us. Tell us about the insights you take from this edition and trends you wish we would cover next time. Email us at trendbook@nais.org. We always love to hear from you.

Myra McGovern is vice president of media at NAIS.

Karla Taylor is co-editor of the *Trendbook*.

The
ECONOMIC
Outlook

By Joseph Corbett

Joseph Corbett is a research analyst at NAIS.

TRENDING
FOR 2021-2022

- After peaking during the early months of the COVID-19 pandemic in 2020, the unemployment rate declined rapidly. But it remains higher for some groups.

- Economic growth rebounded quickly after the initial COVID shutdown. However, almost half of workers reported a loss of income between March 2020 and April 2021.

- Although some obstacles remain, economists and consumers are optimistic that jobs and economic output will continue to recover through the remainder of calendar year 2021.

The COVID-19 pandemic resulted in one of the fastest collapses and one of the most dramatic recoveries the U.S. economy has ever experienced. In February and March 2020, as the virus spread around the world, the U.S. stock market plunged, and the United States was thrust into a recession. The unemployment rate peaked in April 2020, and the gross domestic product (GDP) dropped by nearly one-third in just a few months.

But since the second quarter of 2020, economic indicators have rebounded. Employment has improved markedly since April 2020. GDP also improved quickly, returning to its pre-pandemic level by mid-2021. These trends have helped build optimism among economists and the general public that the U.S. economy will continue to grow as vaccines have become available and the country recovers from the pandemic.

Within that recovery, however, are some worrying signals. Overall, unemployment remains above pre-pandemic levels. In addition, consistent with long-term patterns, unemployment remains significantly higher for those with less education and for Black and Hispanic workers. And a large number of workers—including families with children—report losing income during the past year, particularly workers of color and lower-income workers.

What remains to be seen is whether the loss of many lower-income jobs and potential workforce shifts will result in permanent changes to sectors such as hospitality and food service. For independent schools, these trends signal the need to adjust strategy to meet enrollment and financial goals in the years ahead.

Unemployment Rates Declined Rapidly But Remain High for Some Groups[1]

More than a year after the start of the pandemic, unemployment looked much less dire, decreasing by a significant margin from its initial spike. After reaching a high of 14.8% in April 2020, the unemployment rate began a sharp decline and was 5.9% by June 2021 (Figure 1).

This is starkly different from the Great Recession of 2007-2009, when the percentage of unemployed workers grew more slowly but recovery took signifi-

FIGURE 1: **National Unemployment Rate, January 2020 Through June 2021**

Source: U.S. Bureau of Economic Analysis

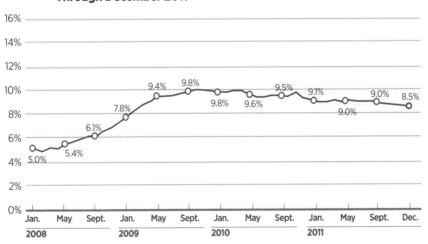

FIGURE 2: **National Unemployment Rate, January 2008 Through December 2011**

Source: U.S. Bureau of Economic Analysis

cantly longer. The unemployment rate grew over almost two years (from 2008 to 2010) and peaked in October 2010 (Figure 2). It did not return to less than 6% until September 2014, almost four years after the peak.

In contrast, unemployment resulting from the pandemic has declined rapidly since the peak in April 2020, falling below 6% just over a year later. This is a positive development. Nevertheless, three factors make the outlook somewhat cloudy as of the summer of 2021.

Overall unemployment remained relatively high. In summer 2021, the unemployment rate was still almost 2.5 percentage points higher than its pre-recession level. In addition, the rate of decrease slowed after the 2020 holiday season. It remains to be seen whether unemployment will return to pre-recession levels soon or whether the United States has entered a "new normal" state.

Unemployment was higher for those with less education. According to the U.S. Bureau of Economic Analysis, level of education strongly correlates with unemployment rates. As in the 2007-2009 recession, individuals without high school diplomas were hardest hit during the pandemic. Those with college degrees saw the smallest increase in unemployment.

The unemployment rate for those without a high school diploma peaked at 21% in April 2020, compared to 15% for those with some college experience or an associate's degree and just 8.4% for those with a bachelor's degree or higher.

By June 2021, the unemployment rate was still over 10% for those without a high school diploma. Those with some college or an associate's degree had an unemployment rate of 5.8%, while those with a bachelor's degree or higher had an unemployment rate of just 3.5% (Figure 3).

FIGURE 3: Unemployment by Level of Education, April 2020 and June 2021

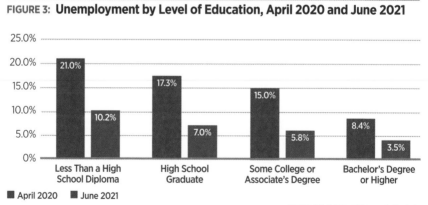

Source: U.S. Bureau of Economic Analysis

FIGURE 4: Unemployment by Race and Ethnicity, April 2020 and June 2021

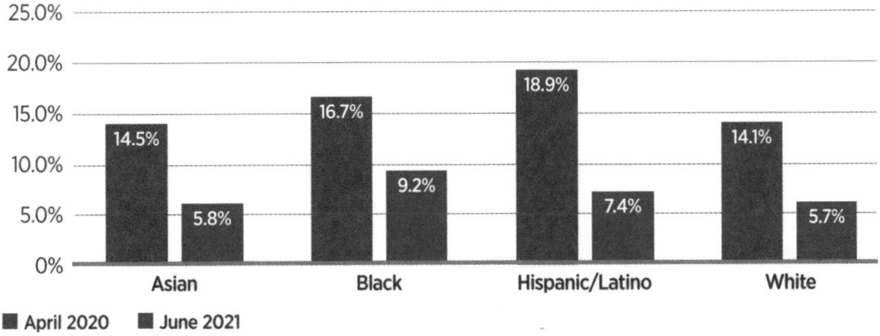

Source: U.S. Bureau of Economic Analysis

Unemployment also varied widely for different racial and ethnic groups. In April 2020, the unemployment rate for white and Asian workers peaked at 14.1% and 14.5%, respectively, compared to 16.7% and 18.9% for Black and Hispanic workers, respectively.

This disparity continued. In June 2021, unemployment rates for white and Asian workers were several percentage points lower than for Black and Hispanic workers (Figure 4).

GDP Has Rebounded, But Many Workers Report Income Losses Over the Past Year

GDP decreased significantly during the initial months of the pandemic, but it returned to a normal level in the following months.

According to the U.S. Bureau of Economic Analysis, GDP fell at an annual rate of more than 31% during the second quarter of 2020. This is a massive drop. The largest decrease in any quarter during the Great Recession of 2007-2009 was only 8.4%.[2]

However, the change brought on by the pandemic was short-lived. GDP went on to grow by an annual rate exceeding 33% in the third quarter of 2020 and increased at a 4.3% annual rate during the fourth quarter (Figure 5). GDP continued to grow strongly in the first half of 2021. In contrast, GDP was negative for an entire year during the 2007-2009 recession, as opposed to half a year for the current recession (Figure 6).[3]

Notably, much of the difference in recovery time can be attributed to per-

FIGURE 5: Real GDP Percent Change from Previous Quarter, Q2 2019 to Q2 2021

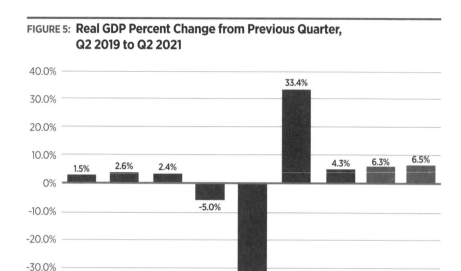

Source: U.S. Bureau of Economic Analysis

FIGURE 6: Real GDP Percent Change from Previous Quarter, Q2 2008 to Q1 2010

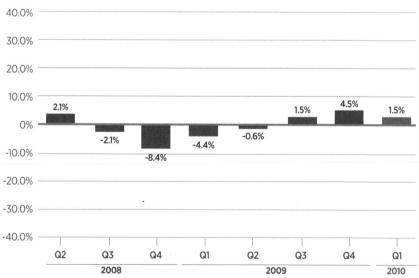

Source: U.S. Bureau of Economic Analysis

sonal consumption habits; consumers were much quicker to resume spending during the COVID-19 crisis than during the Great Recession. This signals a level of confidence in the economy that was not present in the 2007-2009 recession and bodes well for a continued recovery.[4]

Despite these positive changes, causes for concern remain.

Many workers, including some parents, reported lost income over the previous year. The Congressional Research Service reports that "close to half of all households in the United States experienced at least some loss of employment income since March 2020, when the economic effects of the pandemic first became apparent."[5]

Households with lower annual incomes and children were more likely to have experienced a loss of income during 2020 than those with higher incomes (Figure 7). Sixty-five percent of households with children making less than $25,000 and 62% of those making $25,000 to $34,999 experienced a loss of income between March 13, 2020, and late September through mid-October 2020 (when respondents were surveyed).

In contrast, 38% of households making $150,000 to $199,999, and 30% of households making over $200,000, lost income over the same period.[6] Despite wealthier families being less likely to have lost income, the percentage of higher-income households that have lost income over the past year is significant.

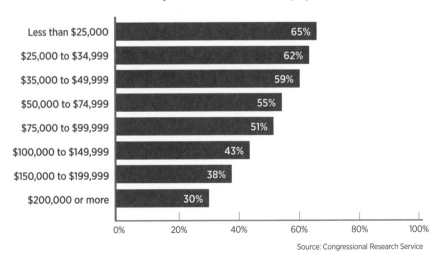

FIGURE 7: **Percentage of Households with Children Losing Income Between March 2020 and September-October 2020, by Income Bracket**

- Less than $25,000: 65%
- $25,000 to $34,999: 62%
- $35,000 to $49,999: 59%
- $50,000 to $74,999: 55%
- $75,000 to $99,999: 51%
- $100,000 to $149,999: 43%
- $150,000 to $199,999: 38%
- $200,000 or more: 30%

Source: Congressional Research Service

Schools may find that investing in tuition is more challenging for all families in 2021, 2022, and perhaps beyond.

Income data by race and ethnicity reveal disparities similar to those found in employment numbers. Hispanic and multiracial workers have been more likely than others to be affected by the pandemic, with 58% and 54% reporting income loss in the past year, respectively. White workers were the least likely to be affected, with 41% reporting a loss of income over the past year (Figure 8).[7] These changes are important for schools to keep in mind when considering the diversity of their student body in the coming years.

Economists and Consumers Are Optimistic About the Economic Future, But Obstacles to Recovery Remain

Economists are hopeful that the recovery will continue, predicting positive changes in GDP during the fourth quarter of 2021. A survey conducted by the National Association for Business Economics (NABE) in April 2021 reveals this optimism: 95% of respondents said they believed that GDP would grow by 3% or more through the first quarter of 2022.[8] This number is often cited as a benchmark for healthy growth in a modern economy and is good news for workers and business owners alike.

Senior fellows at the Brookings Institution take this view further, stating that the "consensus is that real GDP will increase about 6% between the fourth quarter of 2020 and the fourth quarter of 2021." Furthermore, they find that if these estimates are accurate, the U.S. will record average employment gains "between 700,000 and 1 million [jobs] per month, a lot faster than many forecasters

FIGURE 8: Percentage of Workers Losing Income Between March 2020 and September-October 2020, by Race and Ethnicity

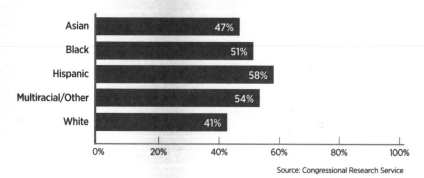

Source: Congressional Research Service

anticipate."[9] In fact, as of July 2021, GDP has grown faster than the Brookings forecast; job growth, however, has been more muted.

Consumers share this optimism. The Conference Board's Consumer Confidence Index began to surge in March 2021, after a modest increase in February. The index has increased since then: The June confidence index was at 127.3, up from 90.4 in February 2021. Consumer confidence took a much longer time to rebound after the 2007-2009 recession: The index did not reach 120 until 2017.[10]

Despite this optimism, challenges remain for the recovery ahead.

Pandemic-driven changes to businesses could affect recovery. Business adaptations during the pandemic, such as working from home, may affect sectors that depend on commuters in central business districts (transit, restaurants, etc.).[11] Changes like these may disproportionately affect lower-income employees who lost work during the pandemic. It is unclear how many of these jobs will return. Also unclear is the potential impact of migration—both people moving out of and into certain areas (as discussed in Chapter 2, "The Demographic Outlook")—on local economies.

Unemployment rates may be underreported. Furthermore, the Pew Research Center reports that decreasing labor force participation rates could mean that more Americans are out of work than the official unemployment rate suggests. The chair of the Federal Reserve Board has suggested that "those who left the labor force since February 2020 should be counted among the unemployed to gain a better understanding of the slump in the labor market." Adjusting for these exits may put the unemployment rate for February 2021 as high as 9.9%, compared to the official unemployment rate of close to 6%.[12]

Independent schools should be aware of these trends as they set strategy for enrollment management, financial aid, fundraising, and other critical functions of school operations.

 ## Strategic Questions

What impact has the pandemic had on your school's families? How have families from various backgrounds been affected differently? Have certain age, racial/ethnic, or other groups been affected more dramatically? How can your school prioritize diversity in its enrollment process amid the crisis?

How have staff and faculty been affected by the crisis? Have changes in staffing or pay made it harder for them to engage effectively with the school community? How can your school consider staff and faculty needs throughout the 2021-2022 school year?

In what ways is the pandemic affecting the potential market for your school? Are some segments of the population being priced out of your school as a result of unemployment or loss of income? What strategies can you employ to ensure continued interest in attendance for local families?

Is your school in a financial position to lower tuition or to provide additional aid to families in need? If so, how long will your school have the resources to do this? If not, what steps can you take to free up or generate funds for these forms of assistance?

 ## Action Steps

Use NAIS's Market View to learn how your local area has been affected by the crisis. Under the "Research" tab, view data for your local community, and explore the tool to understand how families of different income levels and racial/ethnic backgrounds have been affected in your area.

Using Market View, identify neighborhoods from which to recruit full-pay families and families in need of financial aid. Consider shifting your marketing to better reflect the distribution of prospective families in your area.

Use NAIS's Data and Analysis for School Leadership (DASL) to gain a better understanding of your school's revenues and expenses, including how they have changed in the recent past. Compare these changes to shifts in your community's income and employment to understand how your school can remain sustainable through the crisis and beyond.

Consider your school's unique value proposition and how it is satisfying current and prospective families. Review NAIS's Jobs-to-Be-Done research on parents—which examines why parents enroll their children in independent schools—to understand how your school can better serve families in your community.

 ## Resources

"COVID-19 and the U.S. Economy," Congressional Research Service: https://crsreports.congress.gov/product/pdf/R/R46606

**"COVID-19 Pandemic's Impact on Household Employment and Income,"
Congressional Research Service:**
https://crsreports.congress.gov/product/pdf/IN/IN11457

Economic Data, Federal Reserve Bank of St. Louis:
https://fred.stlouisfed.org/

**"How Many Jobs Is the US Likely to Add This Year?" Louise Sheiner and
Gian Maria Milesi-Ferretti, Brookings Institution:**
https://www.brookings.edu/blog/up-front/2021/03/22/how-many-jobs-is-
the-u-s-likely-to-add-this-year/

"Jobs-to-Be-Done Study on Independent School Parents," NAIS:
https://www.nais.org/articles/pages/research/nais-research-jobs-to-be-done-
study-on-independent-school-parents/

**"Labor Force Statistics from the Current Population Survey," U.S.
Bureau of Labor Statistics:**
https://www.bls.gov/cps/

**"NABE Business Conditions Survey," National Association for Business
Economics:**
https://nabe.com/NABE/Surveys/Business_Conditions_Surveys/
January_2021_Business_Conditions_Survey_Summary.aspx

NAIS Market View:
https://marketview.nais.org/

**"U.S. Labor Market Inches Back from the COVID-19 Shock, But
Recovery Is Far from Complete," Rakesh Kochhar and Jesse Bennett,
Pew Research Center:**
https://www.pewresearch.org/fact-tank/2021/04/14/u-s-labor-market-inches-
back-from-the-covid-19-shock-but-recovery-is-far-from-complete/

ENDNOTES

[1] The source of the data in this section is the U.S. Bureau of Economic Analysis, Employment Data; online at https://www.bea.gov/data/employment/employment-by-industry.

[2] U.S. Bureau of Economic Analysis, "Gross Domestic Product: First Quarter 2021 (Advance Estimate)"; online at https://www.bea.gov/data/gdp/gross-domestic-product.

[3] Ibid.

[4] Ibid.

[5] Congressional Research Service, "COVID-19 Pandemic's Impact on Household Employment and Income," November 9, 2020; online at https://crsreports.congress.gov/product/pdf/IN/IN11457.

[6] Ibid.

[7] Ibid.

[8] National Association for Business Economics, "NABE Business Conditions Survey," April 2021; online at https://nabe.com/NABE/Surveys/Business_Conditions_Surveys/April-2021-Business-Conditions-Survey-Summary.aspx.

[9] Louise Sheiner and Gian Maria Milesi-Ferretti, "How Many Jobs Is the US Likely to Add This Year?" Brookings Institution, March 22, 2021; online at https://www.brookings.edu/blog/up-front/2021/03/22/how-many-jobs-is-the-u-s-likely-to-add-this-year/.

[10] The Conference Board, "Consumer Confidence Increased in June," June 29, 2021; online at https://conference-board.org/data/consumerconfidence.cfm.

[11] Sheiner and Milesi-Ferretti, "How Many Jobs Is the US Likely to Add This Year?"

[12] Rakesh Kochhar and Jesse Bennett, "U.S. Labor Market Inches Back from the COVID-19 Shock, But Recovery Is Far from Complete," Pew Research Center, Fact Tank, April 14, 2021; online at https://www.pewresearch.org/fact-tank/2021/04/14/u-s-labor-market-inches-back-from-the-covid-19-shock-but-recovery-is-far-from-complete/.

The
DEMOGRAPHIC
Outlook

By Amada Torres

**Amada Torres is
vice president of studies,
insights, and research
at NAIS.**

TRENDING
FOR 2021-2022

- Population growth has slowed over the last 10 years. The pandemic may have worsened this trend.

- Younger generations continue to drive the diversification of the United States.

- The COVID-19 pandemic spurred many people to move within the U.S., but patterns vary by generation.

America's demographic changes—some long in coming, some brought on since early 2020 by the COVID-19 pandemic—will have a major influence on independent schools in the years to come.

The 2020 U.S. Census numbers reveal that between 2010 and 2020, fewer births, more deaths, and uneven immigration contributed to the lowest population growth recorded since the 1930s. The 2020 pandemic exacerbated this downward trend, producing a record low growth rate of 0.35%.

However, youth population decline has been mitigated by immigrants and their American-born descendants. This, plus the declining size of the white population, continues to contribute to the rapid diversification of the school-age population. Estimated census data show that almost half of the population under 18 years old were people of color in 2020, and their numbers are expected to increase to more than 53% by 2025.

Unlike those gradual changes, mobility shifts in response to the pandemic have seemed relatively sudden. After two decades in which fewer Americans were relocating, the pandemic prompted 10% of individuals, especially younger adults, to move. Americans left the Northeast and Midwest in favor of the Southeast and Southwest.

Continued awareness of these trends and their impact will help independent school leaders devise strategies to navigate the challenges they may pose and take advantage of the opportunities they can create.

Population Growth Has Stagnated

The much-anticipated 2020 U.S. Census corroborated what some demographers have been expecting: The 2010-2020 decade recorded the smallest population growth in the United States since 1930-1940—just 7.4% (Figure 1).[1]

This trend toward slowing growth is not new. The growth rate of the national population began to dip after 2000 and especially after the Great Recession of 2007-2009. But the 2010s recorded far fewer births and more deaths, plus un-

FIGURE 1: **U.S. Population Growth by Decades, 1790-1800 to 2010-2020**

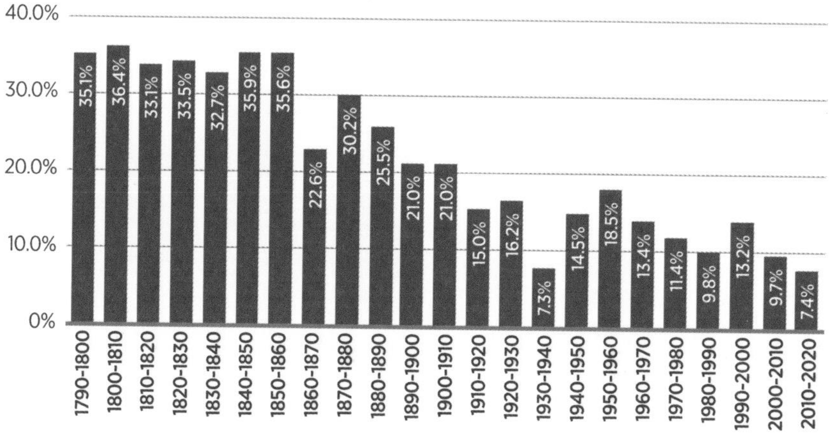

Sources: William H. Frey, "The 2010s Saw the Lowest Population Growth in U.S. History, New Census Estimates Show," Brookings Institution, and Ron Jarmin, "The 2020 Census: Our Growing Nation," U.S. Census Bureau

even immigration, which has been particularly low since 2016-2017. Moreover, the most recent estimated annual population growth (July 2019 to July 2020) reached a mere 0.35%. This is well below the average growth rates over the past 102 years and less than half the level observed in 2000.[2]

Birthrate trends continue to have a significant impact on the potential enrollment market for independent schools. In 2019, the Centers for Disease Control and Prevention (CDC) estimated that there were nearly 3.75 million births in the U.S. This was down 1% from 2018 and constituted the fifth year in a row that the number of births has declined since 2014, when there was an increase. Births fell among women of most races except for Native Hawaiian and Hispanic women.[3]

Total fertility rate (TFR) also declined in 2019 to 1.71 births per woman, even lower than the lowest number in the previous 44 years—1.77 in 1975.[4] This is below "replacement," the level at which a generation can exactly replace itself, generally considered to be 2.1 (Figure 2). The TFR decreased for all racial and ethnic groups except Native Hawaiians. In 2019, the lowest TFRs were registered among non-Hispanic white women, non-Hispanic American Indian women, and non-Hispanic Asian women (Figure 3).[5]

The pandemic has played a role in the most recent decline in births. Researchers estimate that there will be around 300,000 fewer births in 2021 because of the pandemic. Some key elements that influence that forecast include

FIGURE 2: U.S. Total Fertility Rate, 1970-2019

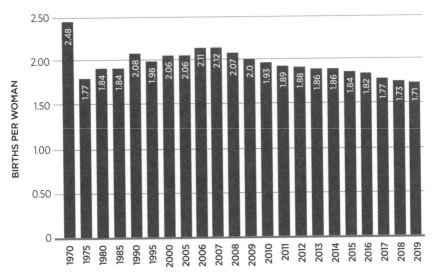

Source: Federal Reserve Bank of St. Louis, "Fertility Rate, Total for the United States"

FIGURE 3: U.S. Total Fertility Rate by Race and Ethnicity, 2016-2019

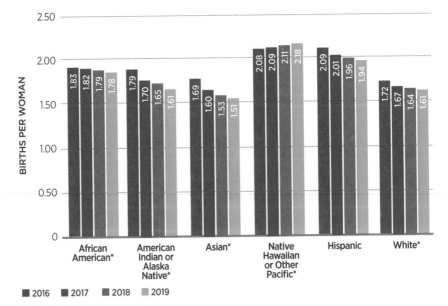

Non-Hispanic members of racial group

Source: Joyce A. Martin et al., "Births: Final Data for 2019," Centers for Disease Control and Prevention

the unemployment rate and the anxiety and social conditions associated with the public health crisis.[6]

Other preliminary reports show how this trend is affecting different parts of the United States. Annual data available from 29 out of the 50 states show that the nation's birthrate in 2020 fell by more than 7%. In December 2020 alone, Hawaii saw 30% fewer births than the previous December, and California saw 10% fewer births.[7]

One of the consequences of lower birthrates is the decreasing representation of children in the U.S. population. In 1960, children represented 35.7% of the total population, compared to 22.1% in 2020. This percentage is projected to continue to decrease to 20.6% by 2040.[8]

A review of selected metro areas where many independent schools are located shows that, by 2025, Baltimore, Boston, Miami, New York, Philadelphia, San Francisco, Seattle, and Washington, DC, will record lower shares of children than the average for the whole country (Table 1).[9] Several economic and societal circumstances are behind these lower birthrates, including increased education and employment opportunities for women, delays in the average age of marriage and childbearing, and the general aging of the population.

Younger Generations Continue to Fuel Diversification

While the child population is not growing as fast as in earlier generations, the number of young people has been sustaining the overall U.S. population and preventing its decline. Estimated data released by the U.S. Census Bureau revealed that, as of July 2019, slightly more than half of the nation's total population (50.7%) were members of the millennial generation or younger (Figure 4).[10]

FIGURE 4: **Share of U.S. Population by Generation, July 2019**

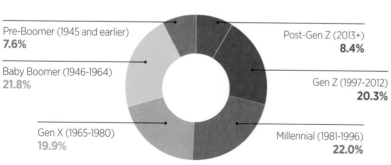

Pre-Boomer (1945 and earlier)
7.6%

Baby Boomer (1946-1964)
21.8%

Gen X (1965-1980)
19.9%

Post-Gen Z (2013+)
8.4%

Gen Z (1997-2012)
20.3%

Millennial (1981-1996)
22.0%

Source: William H. Frey, "Now, More Than Half of Americans Are Millennials or Younger," Brookings Institution

TABLE 1: **Children as a Share of the Population in Selected Metro Areas, 2010, 2020, and 2025 (Projected)**

	2010	2020	2025
Atlanta-Sandy Springs-Alpharetta, GA	26.5%	24.5%	23.3%
Baltimore-Columbia-Towson, MD	23.0%	21.3%	20.2%
Boston-Cambridge-Newton, MA-NH	21.6%	20.0%	19.1%
Bridgeport-Stamford-Norwalk, CT	24.8%	23.0%	22.0%
Charlotte-Concord-Gastonia, NC-SC	25.6%	23.7%	22.6%
Chicago-Naperville-Elgin, IL-IN-WI	25.1%	23.3%	22.2%
Dallas-Fort Worth-Arlington, TX	27.8%	25.8%	24.7%
Denver-Aurora-Lakewood, CO	24.9%	23.3%	22.4%
Detroit-Warren-Dearborn, MI	24.3%	22.5%	21.3%
Los Angeles-Long Beach-Anaheim, CA	24.5%	22.6%	21.6%
Miami-Fort Lauderdale-Pompano Beach, FL	21.7%	19.7%	18.7%
New York-Newark-Jersey City, NY-NJ-PA	22.8%	20.9%	19.8%
Philadelphia-Camden-Wilmington, PA-NJ-DE-MD	23.3%	21.5%	20.4%
San Francisco-Oakland-Berkeley, CA	21.2%	19.8%	18.9%
Seattle-Tacoma-Bellevue, WA	22.8%	21.6%	20.8%
Washington-Arlington-Alexandria, DC-VA-MD-WV	23.9%	22.0%	21.0%
United States	24.0%	22.3%	21.3%

Source: NAIS Demographic Center

In addition to their now larger numbers, a key characteristic of these younger generations is that they are more diverse than previous ones. In 2020, Claritas, a marketing company, estimated that among pre-boomers (people born before 1946) and baby boomers (1946-1964), only 20.7% and 27.7%, respectively, were people of color. That percentage began to rise with Gen X (39.6%) and reached 47.3% for millennials and 51% for Gen Z (Figure 5).[11]

Another interesting difference among the generations is the representation of different racial and ethnic groups. Among pre-boomers and baby boomers, Hispanic and African American people represented similar shares of the population. Among Gen Xers, the gap between Hispanics and African Americans was almost 5 percentage points. And for millennials and Gen Zers, the representation of Hispanics was between 10 and 12 percentages points higher than for African Americans.

The most recent NAIS Demographic Center estimates show that, in 2020,

FIGURE 5: **U.S. Population Distribution by Generation and Race/Ethnicity, 2020**

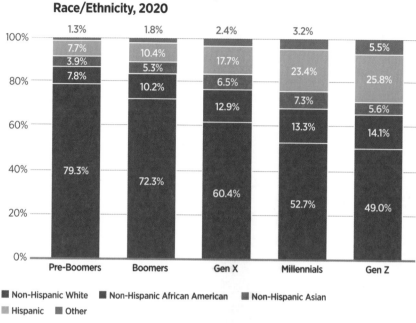

■ Non-Hispanic White ■ Non-Hispanic African American ■ Non-Hispanic Asian
■ Hispanic ■ Other

Source: Claritas, *The 2020 Hispanic Market Report: The New American Mainstream*

nearly half of the population under 18 years old was composed of people of color (49.9%). However, there were stark differences based on metro areas. For example, in Los Angeles, 83.3% of children were people of color. But in Boston, just 36.7% of children were people of color (Figure 6).[12]

Projected numbers for 2025 show that the population under 18 years old will continue to diversify. In 13 of 16 metro areas with large concentrations of independent schools, students of color will make up the majority of the population.[13]

What is behind these changes?

Historically, immigration has been a driving force behind racial and ethnic changes in the United States. Millennials and the generations after them were born during years of higher immigration (1980s through the early 2000s). Increasingly, however, growing racial/ethnic diversity in the United States has been driven by natural increase—the number of births relative to deaths in a population. This has been the case for the growth in the Hispanic population. In contrast, since 2000, the white population under 18 years old has registered absolute population losses.[14]

FIGURE 6: Population of People of Color Under 18 Years of Age, 2020 and 2025 (Projected)

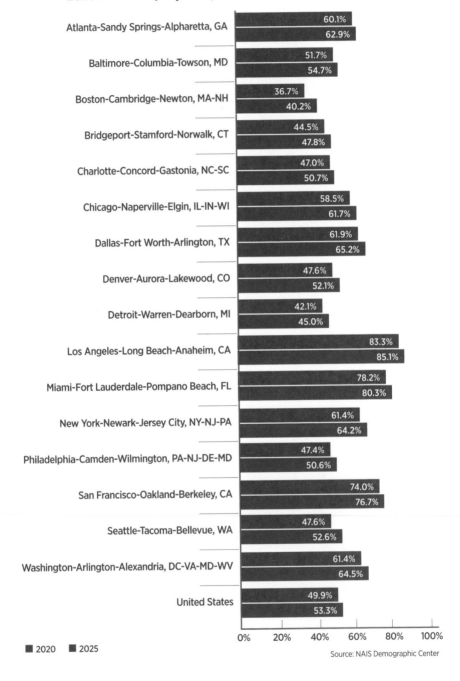

Source: NAIS Demographic Center

The COVID-19 Pandemic Spurred Internal Migration, Especially Among Young Adults

During the last two decades, U.S. mobility rates decreased, especially the year before the pandemic, when they reached a historic low level at 9.3% (Figure 7).[15] While the overall trend was downward, demographers also observed that the drivers of the patterns differed by generation. Among millennials, the internal migration slowdown was due to their postponing buying houses and a weaker job market, especially during the years after the 2007-2009 recession. Millennials also continued to delay marriage and childbearing. Among baby boomers, lower internal migration was largely attributable to delaying retirement or difficulty in selling their homes (among those who wanted to retire and move).[16]

However, there has been much speculation about the impact of the pandemic on moving patterns. Anecdotal information publicized by the news media suggested a COVID-induced migration of residents fleeing some large cities. But an analysis by Bankrate of U.S. Postal Service change-of-address requests during 2020 found that while more people left major cities than moved to them, these movers stayed close. The top five cities losing residents were New York City, Houston, Austin, Orlando, and Dallas. But residents were likely to move to nearby

FIGURE 7: Mobility Rates, 2000-2001 to 2019-2020

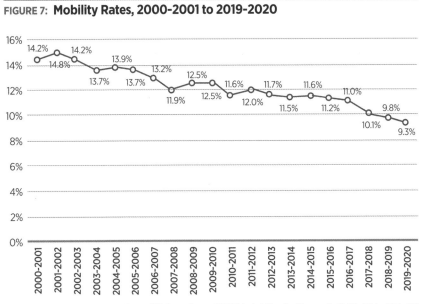

Source: U.S. Census Bureau, "CPS Historical Migration/Geographic Mobility Tables, Table A-1"

suburbs or outlying neighborhoods located between six and 29 miles from these cities—except for individuals who moved from Manhattan to East Hampton (104 miles away) and Southampton (92 miles) on Long Island.[17]

A survey commissioned by Bankrate and conducted by YouGov produced two findings: In 2020, 10% of Americans moved or relocated because of the pandemic. Another 6% moved but then returned. This means that although more people actually moved, the mobility rate ended up being similar to the one recorded in 2017-2018.[18]

The pandemic affected adults in different ways. While some baby boomers decided to retire and move to the South and other new places, young adults ages 18 to 24 (Gen Zers) were more likely than any other age group to have moved

FIGURE 8: Relocation Rates During 2020, by Generation

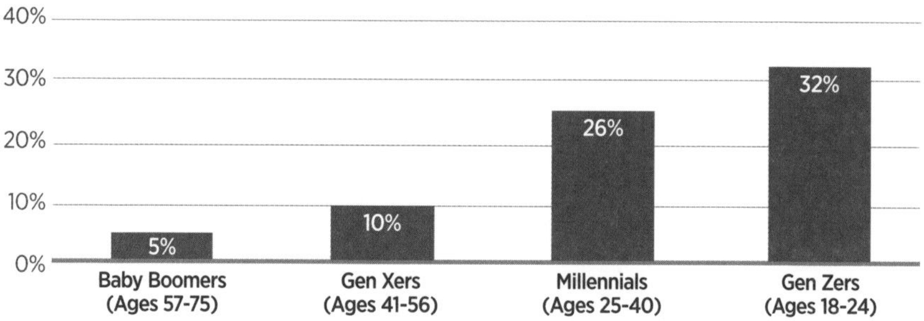

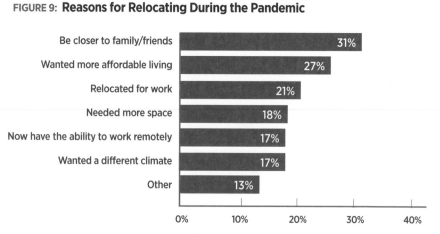

Source: Zach Wichter, "Pandemic Movers Sought Affordability, But Not Too Far Away," Bankrate

FIGURE 9: Reasons for Relocating During the Pandemic

Source: Zach Wichter, "Pandemic Movers Sought Affordability, But Not Too Far Away," Bankrate

TABLE 2: **Inbound and Outbound Migration During 2020**

	Inbound	Outbound	Net Change		Inbound	Outbound	Net Change
Alabama	59.7%	40.3%	19.4%	Montana	51.2%	48.8%	2.4%
Alaska	NA	NA		Nebraska	48.6%	51.4%	-2.8%
Arizona	61.6%	38.4%	23.2%	Nevada	52.4%	47.6%	4.8%
Arkansas	58.5%	41.5%	17.0%	New Hampshire	51.8%	48.2%	3.6%
California	41.3%	58.7%	-17.4%	New Jersey	30.5%	69.5%	-39.0%
Colorado	50.4%	49.6%	0.8%	New Mexico	53.5%	46.5%	7.0%
Connecticut	36.5%	63.5%	-27.0%	New York	33.1%	66.9%	-33.8%
Delaware	57.8%	42.2%	15.6%	North Carolina	60.2%	39.8%	20.4%
Florida	59.6%	40.4%	19.2%	North Dakota	43.3%	56.7%	-13.4%
Georgia	51.0%	49.0%	2.0%	Ohio	43.9%	56.1%	-12.2%
Hawaii	NA	NA		Oklahoma	49.3%	50.7%	-1.4%
Idaho	70.1%	29.9%	40.2%	Oregon	62.5%	37.5%	25.0%
Illinois	33.6%	66.4%	-32.8%	Pennsylvania	46.7%	53.3%	-6.6%
Indiana	46.9%	53.1%	-6.2%	Rhode Island	55.5%	44.5%	11.0%
Iowa	52.1%	47.9%	4.2%	South Carolina	64.0%	36.0%	28.0%
Kansas	41.4%	58.6%	-17.2%	South Dakota	62.3%	37.7%	24.6%
Kentucky	52.4%	47.6%	4.8%	Tennessee	60.0%	40.0%	20.0%
Louisiana	47.3%	52.7%	-5.4%	Texas	54.0%	46.0%	8.0%
Maine	55.7%	44.3%	11.4%	Utah	54.9%	45.1%	9.8%
Maryland	45.0%	55.0%	-10.0%	Vermont	76.6%	23.4%	53.2%
Massachusetts	43.4%	56.6%	-13.2%	Virginia	46.9%	53.1%	-6.2%
Michigan	49.8%	50.2%	-0.4%	Washington	54.5%	45.5%	9.0%
Minnesota	48.8%	51.2%	-2.4%	West Virginia	NA	NA	
Mississippi	48.1%	51.9%	-3.8%	Wisconsin	50.0%	50.0%	0.0%
Missouri	48.8%	51.2%	-2.4%	Wyoming	58.0%	42.0%	16.0%

Source: United Van Lines, "United Van Lines' National Migration Study Reveals Where and Why Americans Moved in 2020"

because of the pandemic (32%). At 26%, millennials were the next largest group who moved (Figure 8). Bankrate's survey identified a desire to be closer to family and friends, more affordable living, and changes in work arrangements as main reasons for relocating during the pandemic (Figure 9).[19]

Internal migration during 2020 also varied by state. A recent study by United

Van Lines, a nationwide moving company, reported that the states with the largest inbound vs. outbound moves were Vermont (53.2%), Idaho (40.2%), South Carolina (28%), and Oregon (25%). States with the largest exoduses included New Jersey (-39%), New York (-33.8%), Illinois (-32.8%), and Connecticut (-27%) (Table 2).[20]

Throughout the pandemic, major metropolitan areas and hotspots, such as New York City, Newark, and Chicago, also experienced greater outbound migration. Lower-density cities like Wilmington, North Carolina, and Boise, Idaho, saw high levels of inbound moves. Generally, migration to western and southern states, a prevalent pattern for the past several years, persisted in 2020.

It is too early to determine how permanent any of these pandemic-related migration patterns will be. Among the factors that could influence these trends are widespread adoption of COVID-19 vaccines, more stable housing markets, a rebounding economy, and increased adoption of telecommuting.

 ## Strategic Questions

As fertility rates continue to decrease, what are the long-term effects on your school? How can you track the direct impact of this trend on your school's enrollment numbers? What strategies can you put in place to mitigate any adverse effects on your ability to meet enrollment goals?

What is the racial and ethnic makeup of your student body and their families? How does the student body compare to the demographic makeup of prospective families in your current and potential markets?

How is the racial and ethnic makeup of your draw area expected to change in the next few years? How should you adapt your admission and marketing strategies to respond to those changes? What programs do you have in place to attract, enroll, and retain families from diverse backgrounds? How do you assess whether your school is addressing individual families' needs? How do you measure their satisfaction and the quality of the student experience?

What mobility patterns are affecting your draw area? How has the pandemic affected relocation patterns among current and prospective families? What emerging neighborhoods are attracting families to your area?

Action Steps

If you are experiencing enrollment challenges, especially in preschool, kindergarten, and lower grade levels, explore partnerships with nursery schools, day cares, and other community organizations in your area to grow a pipeline of young students.

Develop alternative financial scenarios to determine how your school might function if the number of children declines in your area. If the population has shifted or will shift dramatically, consider possible actions such as reconfiguring classes, offering classes based on demand, creating multi-grade classrooms, or increasing class size or adding sections in grade levels with higher demand.

Use NAIS's Data and Analysis for School Leadership (DASL) to evaluate the current ethnic and racial makeup of your school and how it has changed over time. Using NAIS's Market View, compare your school's population to the demographics of your draw area. If you notice opportunities for improvement, explore connections with organizations that have closer ties to underserved communities. Evaluate the ways your school celebrates diversity and embraces families from different backgrounds (for example, through social gatherings, cultural events, affinity groups, volunteer activities) to ensure that all families feel included by your school.

Use NAIS's Market View to track population changes due to mobility patterns in the ZIP codes from which you traditionally attract families. Identify new areas where families are relocating, and evaluate ways to target them. If families are moving farther away, assess opportunities for transportation via bus routes, carpooling, etc. If demand for distance learning continues after the pandemic abates, explore whether you should offer this option via distance learning or an online education consortium.

Review NAIS's research on Jobs to Be Done to build a deeper understanding of why parents choose to enroll (and keep) their children in your school, the implications for your own marketing and admission strategies, and the impact of COVID-19 on parents' wants and needs.

Resources

Brookings Institution, Demographics & Population:
https://www.brookings.edu/topic/demographics-population/

"Jobs-to-Be-Done Study on Independent School Parents," NAIS:

https://www.nais.org/articles/pages/research/nais-research-jobs-to-be-done-study-on-independent-school-parents/

"Managing Enrollment During the Coronavirus Crisis: A Jobs-to-Be-Done Perspective," NAIS:
https://www.nais.org/articles/pages/member/research/managing-enrollment-during-the-coronavirus-crisis-a-jobs-to-be-done-perspective/

NAIS Data and Analysis for School Leadership (DASL):
https://dasl.nais.org/

NAIS Demographic Center:
https://www.nais.org/demographics

NAIS Market View:
https://marketview.nais.org/

"Parents' Jobs to Be Done and COVID-19: What's Changed?" NAIS:
https://www.nais.org/articles/pages/member/research/nais-research-parent-jobs-to-be-done-and-covid-19-changes/

Pew Research Center, Demographics:
https://www.pewresearch.org/topics/demography/

U.S. Census Bureau, Population:
https://www.census.gov/topics/population.html

"Using JTBD in the Admissions Process," NAIS:
https://www.nais.org/getmedia/af92dde5-5605-45cb-915b-b57d6a4479c1/Parent-JTBD-Interview-Guide.pdf

"Using JTBD in Your School's Marketing Messages," NAIS:
https://www.nais.org/getmedia/8a933797-8478-4c7e-b86e-64d54ff936b0/NAIS_Research_Parent_JTBD_Marketing.pdf

ENDNOTES

[1] Ron Jarmin, "The 2020 Census: Our Growing Nation," U.S. Census Bureau, April 2021; online at https://www.census.gov/newsroom/blogs/director/2021/04/2020-census-our-growing-nation.html. William H. Frey, "The 2010s Saw the Lowest Population Growth in U.S. History, New Census Estimates Show," Brookings Institution, December 22, 2020; online at https://www.brookings.edu/blog/the-avenue/2020/12/22/the-2010s-saw-the-lowest-population-growth-in-u-s-history-new-census-estimates-show/. U.S. Census Bureau, "Historical National Population Estimates, July 1, 1900 to July 1, 1999," April 11, 2000, rev. June 28, 2000; online at https://www2.census.gov/programs-surveys/popest/tables/1900-1980/national/totals/popclockest.txt.

[2] Frey, "The 2010s Saw the Lowest Population Growth."

[3] Joyce A. Martin et al., "Births: Final Data for 2019," Centers for Disease Control and Prevention, *National Vital Statistics Reports*, 70, no. 2, March 2021; online at https://www.cdc.gov/nchs/data/nvsr/nvsr70/nvsr70-02-508.pdf.

[4] Federal Reserve Bank of St. Louis, "Fertility Rate, Total for the United States," May 2021; online at https://fred.stlouisfed.org/series/SPDYNTFRTINUSA.

[5] Martin et al., "Births: Final Data for 2019."

[6] Melissa S. Kearney and Phillip Levine, "The Coming COVID-19 Baby Bust: Update," Brookings Institution, December 17, 2020; online at https://www.brookings.edu/blog/up-front/2020/12/17/the-coming-covid-19-baby-bust-update/.

[7] Kate Smith, "The COVID Baby Boom Is Looking More Like a Baby Bust," CBS News, March 3, 2021; online at https://www.cbsnews.com/news/baby-bust-declining-birth-rate-covid-pandemic/.

[8] William H. Frey, "The Demographic Case for Investing in America's Children," Brookings Institution, March 1, 2021; online at https://www.brookings.edu/research/the-demographic-case-for-investing-in-americas-children/.

[9] Author's calculations of several tables from the NAIS Demographic Center.

[10] William H. Frey, "Now, More Than Half of Americans Are Millennials or Younger. Will Their Size and Activism Impact the 2020 Election?" Brookings Institution, July 30, 2020; online at https://www.brookings.edu/blog/the-avenue/2020/07/30/now-more-than-half-of-americans-are-millennials-or-younger/.

[11] Claritas, *The 2020 Hispanic Market Report: The New American Mainstream* (Cincinnati, OH: Claritas, 2020); online at https://claritas.com/resources/2020-hispanic-market-report/.

[12] NAIS Demographic Center, April 2021.

[13] Ibid.

[14] William H. Frey, "What the 2020 Census Will Reveal About America: Stagnating Growth, an Aging Population, and Youthful Diversity," Brookings Institution, January 11, 2021; online at https://www.brookings.edu/research/what-the-2020-census-will-reveal-about-america-stagnating-growth-an-aging-population-and-youthful-diversity/.

[15] U.S. Census Bureau, "CPS Historical Migration/Geographic Mobility Tables, Table A-1. Annual Geographic Mobility Rates, by Type of Movement: 1948-2020," December 2020; online at https://www.census.gov/data/tables/time-series/demo/geographic-mobility/historic.html.

[16] William H. Frey, "How Migration of Millennials and Seniors Has Shifted Since the Great Recession," Brookings Institution, January 31, 2019; online at https://www.brookings.edu/research/how-migration-of-millennials-and-seniors-has-shifted-since-the-great-recession/.

[17] Zach Wichter, "Pandemic Movers Sought Affordability, But Not Too Far Away, USPS Data Shows," Bankrate, March 15, 2021; online at https://www.bankrate.com/real-estate/2020-pandemic-moving-trends-usps-data/.

[18] Ibid.

[19] Ibid.

[20] United Van Lines, "United Van Lines' National Migration Study Reveals Where and Why Americans Moved in 2020," January 4, 2021; online at https://www.unitedvanlines.com/newsroom/movers-study-2020.

The ENROLLMENT Outlook

By Joseph Corbett and Amada Torres

Joseph Corbett is a research analyst at NAIS.

Amada Torres is vice president of studies, insights, and research.

TRENDING
FOR 2021-2022

- Median enrollment has dropped in the wake of the pandemic.

- Smaller schools and schools serving younger students have seen larger pandemic-related decreases in enrollment.

- Despite this, applications and acceptances for the 2021-2022 school year are up.

I n the late summer of 2020, many independent schools reported increased interest in their programs, particularly among families from other types of schools.[1] Given the reported decline in public school enrollment, many media stories speculated that the COVID-19 pandemic would provide an enrollment windfall for private schools.[2] But analyses of NAIS enrollment data show that the total number of independent school students in 2020-2021 was slightly lower than in the 2019-2020 school year, and the median enrollment per school declined in response to the pandemic.[3]

Lower grade levels and smaller schools struggled the most amid the pandemic. For elementary schools and schools with fewer than 300 students, enrollment decreased by several percentage points between 2019-2020 and 2020-2021. For upper grade levels and schools with more than 500 students, enrollment remained virtually unchanged.[4]

Preschools saw the steepest declines throughout the pandemic. This continues the trend of the past decade, when pre-K and lower grade levels lost students as upper divisions grew.[5]

Despite these findings, initial admission numbers for the 2021-2022 school year showed signs of improvement. And a majority of schools reported that applications had increased over the past year. The 2021-2022 school year will tell how many of those applications result in matriculating students.[6]

Median Enrollment Declined During the Pandemic*

Median enrollment per independent school decreased more quickly over the past two years, at least in part because of COVID-19. Median enrollment per school

*Unless otherwise noted, data in this section and the next come from NAIS's Data and Analysis for School Leadership (DASL). Totals may not equal 100% due to rounding.

FIGURE 1: Median Enrollment per School, 2015-2016 to 2020-2021

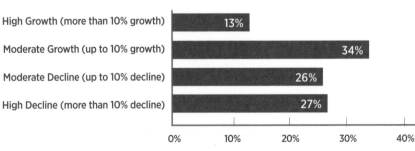

Source: NAIS, Data and Analysis for School Leadership (DASL)

remained fairly stable in the years preceding the pandemic. But it decreased by three students (0.8%) between 2018-2019 and 2019-2020 and then fell by 11 students (2.8%) between 2019-2020 and 2020-2021 (Figure 1). Fifty-three percent of NAIS schools reported a decrease in enrollment over this time period.

Analyzing enrollment by growth category over a five-year period sheds further light on the challenges many independent schools have faced. Between 2015-2016 and 2020-2021, 27% of schools experienced a high enrollment decline (decrease of more than 10%), and 26% saw a moderate decline (decrease of up to 10%) (Figure 2).

But not all schools lost students during this period. More than a third (34%) experienced moderate enrollment growth (increase of up to 10%). A smaller per-

FIGURE 2: School Enrollment Change, 2015-2016 to 2020-2021

Category	Percent
High Growth (more than 10% growth)	13%
Moderate Growth (up to 10% growth)	34%
Moderate Decline (up to 10% decline)	26%
High Decline (more than 10% decline)	27%

Source: NAIS, Data and Analysis for School Leadership (DASL)

centage (13%) experienced high enrollment growth (increase of more than 10%).

These trends are similar to enrollment changes during the Great Recession. From 2006-2007 to 2009-2010, 12.5% of schools experienced a high enrollment decline, and more than 50% experienced enrollment declines in general.

Enrollment Varied by School Type, with Lower Schools and Smaller Schools the Hardest Hit

Different schools experienced enrollment changes differently, depending on a number of variables.

Grade level. Lower schools and lower divisions are struggling more with enrollment than upper schools. Median enrollment for elementary schools was down by 2.6% in 2020-2021 compared to the start of the 2019-2020 school year. But K-12 and upper school median enrollments have remained virtually unchanged or, in some cases, have increased slightly since the start of the pandemic (Figure 3).

School size. The pandemic has had a disproportionate impact on the enrollment of smaller schools. Median enrollment for schools with under 101 students declined more than 5%, and the median decline for schools with 101 to 300 students was just over 4%. In contrast, schools with 501 to 700 students maintained their enrollment. And schools with more than 700 students saw a slight increase between 2019-2020 and 2020-2021 (Figure 4).

FIGURE 3: **Median Enrollment Change per School Grade Range Served, 2019-2020 to 2020-2021**

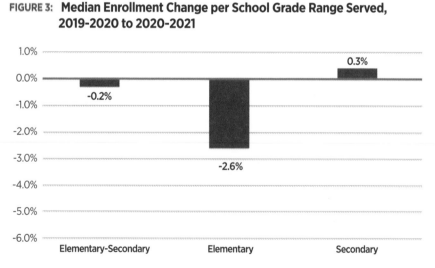

Source: NAIS, Data and Analysis for School Leadership (DASL)

FIGURE 4: **Median Enrollment Change by School Size, 2019-2020 to 2020-2021**

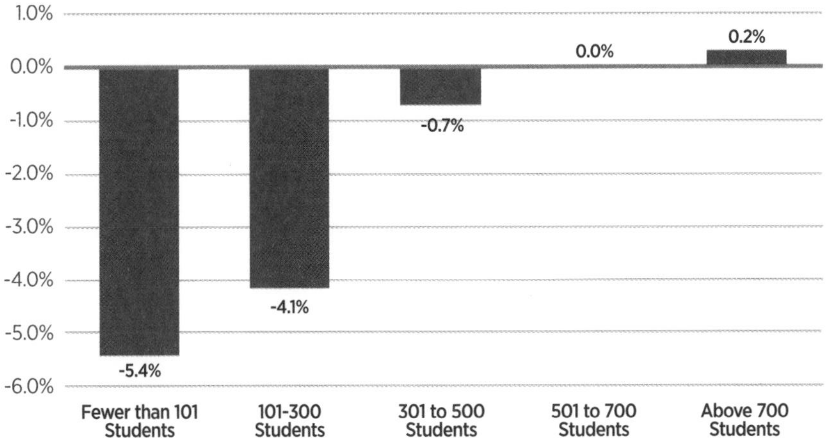

Source: NAIS, Data and Analysis for School Leadership (DASL)

Religious affiliation. Jewish schools fared better than their peers, with a median enrollment increase of 1% between 2019-2020 and 2020-2021. Friends schools struggled, experiencing a 2.2% decrease in median enrollment over the same time period. Schools with other religious affiliations all experienced enrollment declines of less than 1%, while enrollment for nondenominational schools remained the same over the last two years.

A Closer Look at Grade Levels

Because many independent schools depend heavily on the lower grades to supply students to upper divisions, it's worth looking more closely at what's happened in pre-K and the elementary grades, both in the past decade and more recently.

Previous *Trendbook* analyses showed enrollment challenges in the lower grades.[7] Between 2010-2011 and 2015-2016, the total number of students between preschool and third grade decreased. Moreover, during the next five-year period (2015-2016 to 2020-2021), the decline continued and then spread across most lower and middle school grade levels. This decrease contributed to the overall 10-year enrollment drop for all lower school grade levels (preschool to fifth grade), particularly among students in preschool, first, and second grades, each of which recorded a 10% decline (Table 1).

Given this historical trend, many independent school leaders were nervous

TABLE 1: **Changes in the Total Number of Students in Each Grade, 2010-2011 to 2020-2021**

	2010-2011 to 2015-2016	2015-2016 to 2020-2021	Ten-year change (2010-2011 to 2020-2021)
Preschool	-13%	4%	-10%
Kindergarten	-6%	-1%	-7%
1st Grade	-6%	-4%	-10%
2nd Grade	-5%	-5%	-10%
3rd Grade	-1%	-7%	-8%
4th Grade	0%	-5%	-5%
5th Grade	1%	-4%	-3%
6th Grade	5%	-3%	2%
7th Grade	5%	-2%	3%
8th Grade	2%	2%	4%
9th Grade	6%	0%	5%
10th Grade	7%	-1%	6%
11th Grade	4%	2%	7%
12th Grade	4%	3%	7%

Source: NAIS, Data and Analysis for School Leadership (DASL)

when the pandemic hit before families had locked in enrollment plans for the 2020-2021 school year. Layering the economic crisis on top of the health emergency put additional pressure on enrollment goals.

The enrollment disruptions caused by the pandemic were clear when reports came in of large enrollment drops in public schools, especially in the early grade levels, such as preschool and kindergarten. An October 2020 NPR poll of 60 public school districts in 20 states showed an average kindergarten enrollment decline of 16%.[8] A similar analysis of K-12 enrollment across public schools in 33 states conducted by Chalkbeat and the Associated Press in late fall 2020 found that enrollment had dropped by 2% from the previous year. This represented more than 500,000 students.[9]

Across all grades except 12th, the number of students enrolled in independent schools dipped slightly between 2019-2020 and 2020-2021. While schools serving children in kindergarten were most severely affected by the pandemic, the total number of students enrolled in kindergarten remained almost the same, recording just a 0.2% decline. However, preschool enrollment took a

FIGURE 5: Enrollment Change by Grade Level, 2019-2020 to 2020-2021

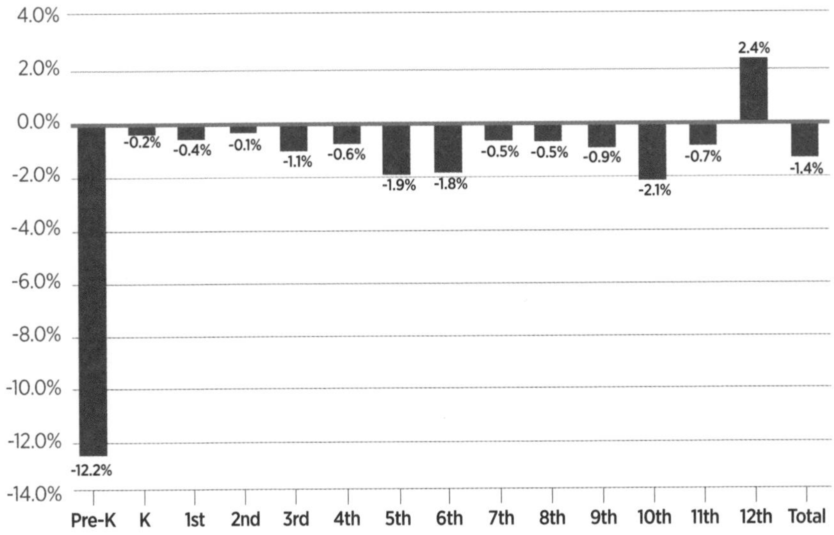

Source: NAIS, Data and Analysis for School Leadership (DASL)

hard hit, recording a 12.2% drop compared to the previous year (Figure 5).

This enrollment decline was not evenly spread among schools. Smaller schools and those located in the Midwest and Mid-Atlantic regions recorded the largest drops in preschool enrollment. The smallest schools (those with fewer than 101 students) were the most likely to experience preschool enrollment declines; 74% of schools with fewer than 101 students had preschool enrollment declines of 10% or more. In contrast, only 36% of large schools (more than 700 students) had preschool enrollment losses that large (Figure 6).

Similarly, 65% of schools located in the Midwest and 60% of those in the Mid-Atlantic region registered enrollment drops greater than 10% among their preschool populations. Schools in the following states recorded significant declines of 10% or more of their preschool enrollment:

- 92% of schools in Missouri
- 81% of schools in Georgia
- 75% of schools in Louisiana
- 72% of schools in California
- 72% of schools in New Jersey

FIGURE 6: Preschool Enrollment Change by School Size, 2019-2020 to 2020-2021

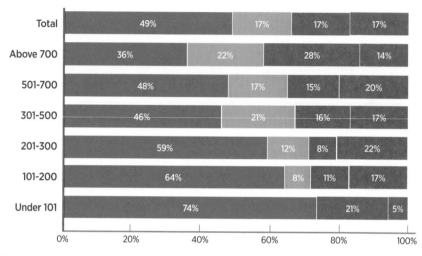

Source: NAIS Snapshot, "Admissions," March 2021

New England was the only region in the country in which more schools reported preschool enrollment increases (53%) than declines (Figure 7).

But again, independent schools were not alone in experiencing enrollment declines during the pandemic. The National Institute for Early Education Research at Rutgers University found that most state-funded pre-K programs reported lower enrollment numbers in fall 2020 than in the previous year. In some states, that decline was as high as 41%. Although enrollment had bounced back somewhat in some states by spring 2021, it continued to be lower than the previous year.[10]

What explains the decline in the number of preschoolers in independent schools during 2020-2021?

Some possible explanations could be the same ones attributed to the "missing" preschool and kindergarten students in public schools. Families may have decided to skip the year altogether because of their concern about the safety of in-person school or the difficulty of navigating remote instruction for pre-K and kindergarten children.[11] Some families opted to switch to less expensive parochial or other private schools, childcare centers, or charter schools. The pandemic also

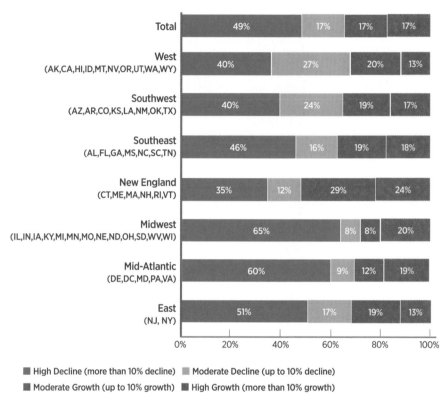

FIGURE 7: Preschool Enrollment Change by Region, 2019-2020 to 2020-2021

Source: NAIS, Data and Analysis for School Leadership (DASL)

sparked interest in homeschooling and other alternative school arrangements. The U.S. Census reported that homeschooling, which had remained around 3.3% since 2012, increased to 5.4% during spring 2020 and to 11.1% by the fall.[12] Although pandemic pods seemed like a good option for some families, a study by *Education Next* at the Harvard Kennedy School found that slightly fewer than 6% of students were participating in a pandemic pod. Twenty percent of these parents were paying for assistance with instruction for a pandemic pod, but this number was significantly higher among higher-income families (39%) than lower-income families (8%).[13]

It is still too early to predict the full impact of COVID-19 on preschool and kindergarten enrollment in independent schools. However, a Snapshot Survey

FIGURE 8: Change in 2021-2022 Pre-K and Kindergarten Applications Compared to Previous Year

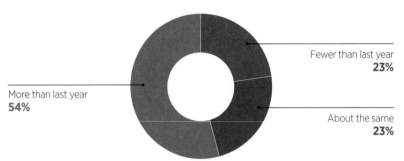

Fewer than last year
23%

More than last year
54%

About the same
23%

Source: NAIS Snapshot, "Admissions," March 2021

that NAIS conducted among admission officers in March 2021 found that 54% of participants' schools had received more applications for those grade levels than the year before (Figure 8). This percentage was even higher (63%) among schools with fewer than 201 students and schools in the New England, Southeast, and Middle Atlantic regions.[14]

Early Indicators Suggest That the Admission Funnel May Improve for 2021-2022

Despite the changes in median enrollment between 2019-2020 and 2020-2021, the majority of independent schools report steady or increasing numbers of applications (73%) and acceptances (83%) since the pandemic began. Thirty-five percent of respondents to the Snapshot Survey experienced an increase in applications of more than 10% in the past year (Figure 9).[15]

Independent schools saw more modest increases in the number of students they accepted during the same period. While 42% of schools reported increases in the number of accepted students, 41% kept the number of accepted students about the same.[16]

Nineteen percent of schools reported higher attrition between 2019-2020 and 2020-2021, while 51% of schools reported fewer families leaving during the same period.[17] Taken together, this information about applicants, acceptances, and attrition suggests that the admissions funnel is moving in the right direction and that the enrollment outlook may improve in the coming academic year.

FIGURE 9: Application and Acceptance Changes, 2019-2020 to 2020-2021

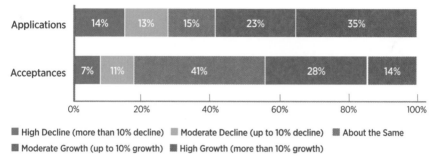

Source: NAIS Snapshot, "Admissions," March 2021

Strategic Questions

How has your school's enrollment changed as a result of the pandemic? In what ways might these trends continue after the pandemic?

How do enrollment patterns differ by grade level in your school? Which specific divisions might need extra attention to ensure steady enrollment in the short and long terms?

How has the number of applications to your school changed since the pandemic began? How have acceptance rates changed? Did these numbers improve as more Americans received COVID vaccinations?

What changes did you make to your application process because of the pandemic? Which ones worked well? Which should you consider keeping or eliminating? How did interactions with families who weren't familiar with independent schools differ from the usual school-family interactions? What lessons have you learned from these interactions?

How have your virtual and modified in-person admissions events gone over? What improvements can your team make to increase the numbers at the top of the admissions funnel? How about contact with accepted students? What improvements could help keep yield up?

What leads families to enroll in your school, and what outcome are they trying to achieve by enrolling? How have the situations families find themselves in changed since the pandemic began? What aspects of their children's school experience during the pandemic worked well? What didn't work? How do these responses vary by grade level? What can your school do to better align its programming and marketing to differentiate it from other schools in your area?

 ## Action Steps

Use NAIS's Market View or similar tools to get a picture of how demographic trends in your area have changed over the past several years and how they're expected to change in the future. Use this information to have strategic discussions regarding enrollment planning over the next several years.

Use NAIS's Data and Analysis for School Leadership (DASL) to evaluate your school's enrollment trends in comparison with peer schools. If your school is experiencing declining enrollment over time, consider possible reasons, including the need to better differentiate your school in the market. Review NAIS's research study *Defining the Role of Independent Schools in the 21st Century Economy* for ideas on how to differentiate your school's offerings.

Review NAIS's Snapshot Surveys for information on how other schools are faring with admissions, COVID policies and vaccinations, and more. These data can help school leaders contextualize the decisions they are making for the community.

If your school serves students in preschool and kindergarten, be prepared to have conversations with families whose children will be entering those grades after being at home during the pandemic. For example, explain your approach to educating children who may have different learning needs, not only in terms of academics but also in terms of social-emotional skills.

Use NAIS's Connect to engage with other schools and to gain context and answers to pressing questions regarding enrollment.

Review your enrollment by grade level and division. Evaluate whether there are grade levels to target with outreach, and consider ways to do so in the current environment. If certain grade levels are suffering because of larger demographic trends, consider ways to manage lower enrollment overall, such as creating combined or multi-grade classrooms or increasing class size in grades with higher demand to compensate financially.

Review NAIS's research on Jobs to Be Done to build a deeper understanding of why parents choose to enroll (and keep) their children in your school. From the "Jobs" profiles provided, evaluate which one or two your school primarily serves. Assess how the pandemic may have created a new context in which you need to meet parents' needs. Consider how your program and marketing appeal to families in these Jobs and what changes may help solidify that appeal.

 ## Resources

***Defining the Role of Independent Schools in the 21st Century Economy*, NAIS:**
https://www.nais.org/getmedia/dfdaaf8b-1c9d-4e82-8aba-d5f417a9098a/NAIS_Research_Role_of_Independent_Schools_21st_Century_Economy.pdf

"Jobs-to-Be-Done Study on Independent School Parents," NAIS:
https://www.nais.org/articles/pages/member/research/nais-research-jobs-to-be-done-study-on-independent-school-parents/

NAIS Connect:
https://connect.nais.org/home

NAIS Data and Analysis for School Leadership (DASL):
https://dasl.nais.org/

***The NAIS Enrollment Management Handbook: A Comprehensive Guide for Independent Schools*, Christine Hailer Baker (ed.), NAIS:**
https://my.nais.org/s/store#/store/browse/detail/a133m000008Hyl9AAC

NAIS Market View:
https://marketview.nais.org/

NAIS Snapshot Surveys:
https://www.nais.org/articles/pages/member/research/nais-snapshot-survey/

ENDNOTES

[1] NAIS, "2020-2021 Enrollment," NAIS Snapshot, Week of August 10, 2020; online at https://www.nais.org/getmedia/87bdaa62-07c3-4509-9cae-373fd48e5042/NAIS-Snapshot-Survey_Enrollment_08-14-20.pdf.

[2] Anya Kamenetz, Marco A. Treviño, and Jessica Bakeman, "Enrollment Is Dropping in Public Schools Around the Country," NPR, October 9, 2020; online at https://www.npr.org/2020/10/09/920316481/enrollment-is-dropping-in-public-schools-around-the-country.

[3] NAIS, Data and Analysis for School Leadership (DASL).

[4] Ibid.

[5] Ibid.

[6] Ibid.

[7] Joseph Corbett and Amada Torres, "The Enrollment Outlook," *2019-2020 NAIS Trendbook* (Washington, DC: NAIS, 2019).

[8] Kamenetz et al., "Enrollment Is Dropping in Public Schools."

[9] Kalyn Belsha et al., "Across U.S., States See Public School Enrollment Dip as Virus Disrupts Education," Chalkbeat, December 22, 2020; online at https://www.chalkbeat.org/2020/12/22/22193775/states-public-school-enrollment-decline-covid.

[10] Allison H. Friedman-Krauss et al., *The State of Preschool 2020: State Preschool Yearbook* (New Brunswick, NJ: National Institute for Early Education Research, Rutgers Graduate School of Education, 2021); online at https://nieer.org/wp-content/uploads/2021/04/YB2020_Full_Report.pdf.

[11] Ibid.

[12] Casey Eggleston and Jason Fields, "Census Bureau's Household Pulse Survey Shows Significant Increase in Homeschooling Rates in Fall 2020," U.S. Census Bureau, March 22, 2021; online at https://www.census.gov/library/stories/2021/03/homeschooling-on-the-rise-during-covid-19-pandemic.html?utm_campaign=20210322msacos1ccstors&utm_medium=email&utm_source=govdelivery.

[13] Michael B. Henderson, Paul E. Peterson, and Martin R. West, "Pandemic Parent Survey Finds Perverse Pattern: Students Are More Likely to Be Attending School in Person Where Covid Is Spreading More Rapidly," *Education Next,* Harvard Kennedy School, Spring 2021; online at https://www.educationnext.org/pandemic-parent-survey-finds-perverse-pattern-students-more-likely-to-be-attending-school-in-person-where-covid-is-spreading-more-rapidly/.

[14] NAIS, "Admissions," NAIS Snapshot, Week of March 29, 2021; online at https://www.nais.org/getmedia/918ebe00-d6d2-4a5e-a51d-ea94a56d181a/NAISsnapshotSurvey040221admissions.pdf.

[15] Ibid.

[16] Ibid.

[17] Ibid.

The
AFFORDABILITY
AND DEMAND
Outlook

by Mark J. Mitchell

Mark J. Mitchell is a vice president at NAIS.

TRENDING
FOR 2021-2022

- The pandemic exacerbated challenges to affordability and access, but most schools did not lower their tuition.

- Many schools offered additional financial aid to help families during the pandemic but to a lesser degree than seen in the Great Recession of 2007-2009.

- Many families switched school types during the crisis, moving among public schools, private schools, and homeschooling.

Despite the pandemic's substantial impact on independent schools—as well as on all types of education—some things did not change. Before the pandemic took hold in March 2020, most independent schools had already announced their 2020-2021 tuition. In the vast majority of cases, that tuition was an increase over 2019-2020. And the majority of schools stayed with that tuition even as COVID-19 caused many schools to adapt to online teaching.

But many other aspects of access, affordability, and demand shifted in 2020-2021, often in surprising ways. Many schools sought to help families by increasing the availability of financial aid, but the number of aid applications from low-income families fell compared to past years. And schools tried to keep up with a great deal of "switching behavior" among families who shifted among independent schools, public schools, and homeschooling.

The full impact of the pandemic probably won't be evident for some time to come. But one thing is certain: In a year like no other, schools' ability to adapt was put to the test.

The Pandemic Exacerbated Challenges to Access and Affordability, But Most Schools Did Not Lower Tuition*

Although schools continued to be concerned about affordability, access, and—for some—sustainability, reducing tuition was not an option for most during the pandemic.

Making significant adjustments to tuition was not the primary way most schools sought to address the potential economic effects of the COVID-19

---

*Unless otherwise noted, data in this chapter come from NAIS's Data and Analysis for School Leadership (DASL).

crisis on families. In July 2020, only 5% of the schools responding to an NAIS Snapshot Survey reported lowering tuition for 2020-2021 because of the pandemic.[1] The vast majority (88.8%) of day schools reported that the pandemic did not affect their tuition and fees for the 2020-2021 year. However, boarding-day schools were more likely to have flexed their list prices, with almost a fifth (17.6%) reporting that they adjusted their tuition as a result of the pandemic. These responses suggest that tuition decisions for most schools largely followed the same patterns in place before the pandemic.

Before the pandemic began, most day schools had raised their 2020-2021 tuition by more than in past years. Among day schools, the median tuition for all grades grew 4.1% between 2019-2020 and 2020-2021, compared to 3.1% average annual growth in the previous five years (Figure 1). There was notable variability in tuition increases by grade level in day school tuition. Preschool tuition and fees grew the least, at just 1.3% over 2019-2020 (about half the typical annual growth rate in the previous five years for this grade). Meanwhile, the median ninth grade tuition grew the most, at 4.4%.

Median boarding tuition and fees among boarding-day schools grew 3.2% between 2019-2020 and 2020-2021, compared to an average of 3% per year between 2015-2016 and 2019-2020. However, day tuition and fees at boarding-day schools grew more modestly between 2019-2020 and 2020-2021 at 2.3%. These

---

FIGURE 1: **Percentage Change in Tuition, 2015-2016 to 2019-2020 and 2019-2020 to 2020-2021**

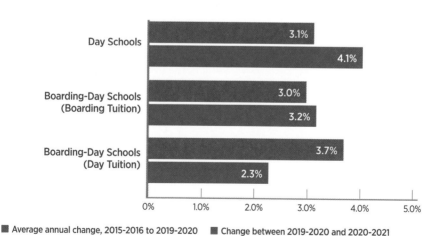

Source: NAIS, Data and Analysis for School Leadership (DASL)

percentages compare to 3.7% average annual growth in the previous five years and to 4.1% growth in tuition at day schools between 2019-2020 and 2020-2021. This could reflect a pandemic-driven effort among boarding-day schools to attract more local domestic students in anticipation of waning enrollment of boarders as parents became reluctant to send their children away from home. Schools with substantial international enrollment also faced challenges when their students were unable to return to the U.S. because of COVID travel restrictions.[2]

Many Schools Offered Additional Financial Aid

Instead of adjusting tuition to address the pandemic's economic effects on families, many schools offered more aid or created new forms of financial assistance. Ninety percent of the schools responding to a May 2020 NAIS Snapshot Survey had taken action to assist families who were financially impacted by the COVID-19 crisis. More than half (57%) of the schools reported that they had created emergency grant funds to support families' short-term, one-time needs. Nearly four in 10 schools (37%) had increased their general financial aid budgets for 2020-2021 in anticipation of the pandemic's financial impact. The additional funding came from specific fundraising efforts, reduced or reallocated operating expenses, or board allocation of endowment or reserve funds.[3] In an acknowledgment of the difficulties families were still experiencing in planning during the pandemic, a small percentage (9%) who responded to a March 2021 NAIS Snapshot Survey reported that they had extended the deadline for 2021-2022 financial aid applications, and 1% had eliminated the deadline altogether.[4]

    Even though many schools increased their aid coffers, demand for financial aid increased far less dramatically than during the Great Recession of 2007-2009. Among boarding-day schools, the median number of financial aid recipients grew just 1.9% in 2020-2021 over 2019-2020 (Figure 2). Even at this low rate of growth, the increase does register as a spike compared to the average annual growth in aid recipients of 0.7% over the previous five years.

    In day schools, a similar pattern played out: 3.3% more students on average received financial aid in 2020-2021 over the previous year, compared to an average annual *decrease* of 0.3% over the previous five years. While an increase in aid recipients in the COVID-driven economy may be unsurprising, it is notable that this growth fell far short of the increases in aid demand schools experienced in the 2007-2009 recession, which saw as many as 17.8% more aid recipients in day schools in 2009-2010 over the 2008-2009 school year.[5] One reason for this may be the rapid economic recovery during the pandemic. Economic recovery was very slow after the Great Recession with unemployment rates remaining high through 2011. In contrast, unemployment rose sharply at the beginning of the pandemic, but almost immediately began to fall from the peak of 14.8% in April 2020 to 5.9% in June 2021[6] (see Chapter 1, "The Economic Outlook").

The increase in aid recipients in 2020-2021 led to an increase in total financial aid spending. Notably, though, the total aid spending grew faster than the growth in average grants that families received. This suggests that many of the new financial aid recipients and applicants came from higher-income families with less financial need.

In day schools, the median total amount of aid granted for 2020-2021 was up 5% over 2019-2020, compared to average annual growth of 4.2% in the previous five years. In boarding-day schools, median aid spending grew 4.2% in 2020-2021, a slowdown from the average annual growth of 5.4% in the previous half

FIGURE 2: Percentage Change in Financial Aid Demand, 2015-2016 to 2019-2020 and 2019-2020 to 2020-2021

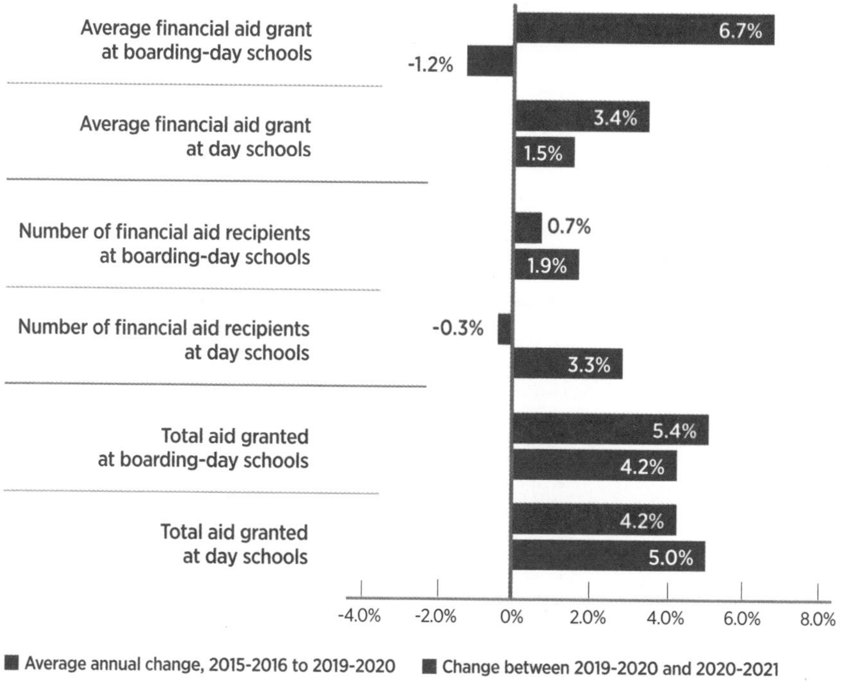

Average financial aid grant at boarding-day schools: 6.7% / -1.2%
Average financial aid grant at day schools: 3.4% / 1.5%
Number of financial aid recipients at boarding-day schools: 0.7% / 1.9%
Number of financial aid recipients at day schools: -0.3% / 3.3%
Total aid granted at boarding-day schools: 5.4% / 4.2%
Total aid granted at day schools: 4.2% / 5.0%

■ Average annual change, 2015-2016 to 2019-2020   ■ Change between 2019-2020 and 2020-2021

Source: NAIS, Data and Analysis for School Leadership (DASL)

decade. Meanwhile, the median financial aid grant grew just 1.5% in day schools (compared to 3.4% average annual growth previously) and actually went *down* among boarding-day schools compared to its recent trending (-1.2% vs. 6.7%).

Fewer low-income families applied for financial aid. Recent trends in financial aid demand by family income show that since 2017, the median number of financial aid applications from families earning below $75,000 has dropped at day schools. In contrast, applications from families earning $75,000 to $150,000 have held mostly steady, and applications from those earning more than $150,000 have increased (Figure 3).

FIGURE 3: Median Number of Financial Aid Applications per Day School, by Family Income, 2017-2018 to 2020-2021

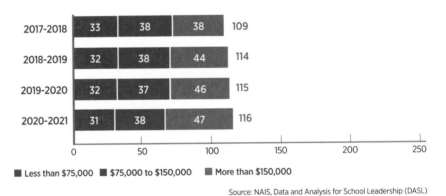

Source: NAIS, Data and Analysis for School Leadership (DASL)

FIGURE 4: Median Number of Financial Aid Applications per Boarding-Day School, by Family Income, 2017-2018 to 2020-2021

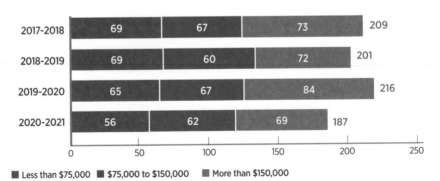

Source: NAIS, Data and Analysis for School Leadership (DASL)

The trend of a declining number of lower-income financial aid applicants is especially present in boarding-day schools, while the trend among applicants from other income levels is more varied (Figure 4). Decreased representation of low-income families in the aid applicant pool appears to have continued for the 2021-2022 school year as well.

According to School and Student Services (SSS) financial aid applicant data comparing October 2020 through March 2021 to the same period in the previous school year, there was a 32% drop in the number of applications for the 2021-2022 year from families eligible for fee waivers.[7] One possible explanation: Lower-income families are waiting longer to engage in—or are postponing—the private school search process because of the pandemic's disproportionate impact on their lives and the uncertain future.

The decline in lower-income families in the aid applicant pool mirrors the trend in higher education. Through January 2021, the number of high school seniors completing the Free Application for Federal Student Aid (FAFSA) was down overall by nearly 10% from the previous year, driven by a 12.4% decrease in applications from students attending Title I-eligible high schools.[8] A contributing factor may be that school closures and remote environments through the fall and winter left students with little or no access to the advising services that many low-income families, in particular, rely on to complete the search process. This may also be true for many lower-income students who attend public schools and didn't have the needed support to explore independent school options.

The unpredictability of virus "surges" during 2020 also undoubtedly played a role in families' reluctance—or inability—to consider making such a significant financial investment during a time of great uncertainty.

Many Families Switched School Types During the Pandemic

Attrition rates have been trending upward in many independent schools since 2015-2016. However, attrition was significantly higher in 2020-2021, particularly among elementary day schools.

School switching was one factor in attrition rates in 2020-2021 for all types of schools and especially for younger children. As parents struggled to deal with often-abrupt school closings, as well as health and safety concerns for their children, they demonstrated considerable "switching behavior." By October 2020, 22% of the families responding to an EdChoice poll had switched the type of school their children attended. Parents of the youngest students were most likely to have switched schools, with more than a quarter (27%) of those with children in kindergarten through fourth grade having done so. Meanwhile, 23% of parents with children in grades five through eight and just 12% of parents of high school students changed their children's schools.[9]

Concern for their children's safety during the pandemic caused 43% of the public school parents who switched to opt for homeschooling during the pandemic. Of all parents who switched schools, 7% of them moved from a private school to their public district school; 5% moved to homeschooling; and just 1% moved to a public charter school (Table 1).[10]

Among those who switched to a private school, 13% moved from a public district school; 4% switched from homeschooling; and 4% left a public charter school. Notably, parents who switched were nearly twice as likely to move from a public district school to a private school (13%) than from a private school to their district's public option (7%).[11]

TABLE 1: **Students Switching Among School Types, 2020**

FROM School Type Attended in 2019-2020	% of total switching	TO School Type Attended in 2020-2021
Home school	4%	Private school
Home school	1%	Public charter school
Home school	7%	Public district school
Private school	5%	Home school
Private school	1%	Public charter school
Private school	7%	Public district school
Public charter school	7%	Home school
Public charter school	4%	Private school
Public charter school	2%	Public district school
Public district school	43%	Home school
Public district school	13%	Private school
Public district school	6%	Public charter school

Source: EdChoice, "October 2020 General Population Polling Presentation"

More parents chose homeschooling as a safer alternative for their children. Within independent schools, an NAIS Snapshot Survey conducted in January 2021 with admission professionals found that nearly half (49%) of respondents reported that they observed more families opting for homeschooling than at the same time the previous year. Much smaller percentages saw more families switching to public schools or another independent school (16% and 12%, respectively). Mirroring the pattern in the EdChoice survey, independent school respondents noted that switching among parents with younger children was more common, with 63% of elementary school respondents seeing more families opting for homeschooling compared to 19% of secondary school respondents.[12]

It will be important for independent schools to track how many of these families return to independent schools as more parents resume in-person work. For independent schools, families' increased willingness to try new options presents many opportunities.

Strategic Questions

What lessons about affordability and demand did your school learn through the pandemic?

What factors throughout the pandemic most affected families' *ability* to pay your tuition? What factors most affected families' *willingness* to pay your tuition? How did you respond to these factors? What might you do differently when the next "black swan event" occurs?

What retention strategies did your school employ to retain students and families who chose your school as a result of the pandemic?

What systems or processes for tuition setting might you change as a result of the pandemic?

What systems or processes for financial aid budgeting or awarding might you change because of the pandemic?

Action Steps

Engage in a deep-dive planning session with your school's enrollment management team to evaluate and fully understand the impact of the pandemic, for better or worse, on your enrollment and affordability goals. Be intentional about the ways you attempt to reengage with families who left your school for other options during the pandemic.

Develop a strategic retention plan specifically for families who switched to your school during the pandemic. Be intentional about the ways you attempt to keep them engaged with you when other options open up for them.

Read the resources in the NAIS "Reimagine Tuition" series to engage your board and leadership team in rethinking pricing and financial aid strategies. Consider new approaches and models for keeping pandemic-driven tuition growth moderation part of your longer-term strategy for affordability.

 ## Resources

NAIS Data and Analysis for School Leadership (DASL):
https://dasl.nais.org

NAIS Market View:
https://marketview.nais.org

Reimagine Tuition: A Decision-Making Process for School Leaders, Mark J. Mitchell, NAIS:
https://www.nais.org/getmedia/2528339f-179b-43b8-854f-4dd179b81131/RethinkingTuition_12-22-20F.pdf

Reimagine Tuition: Is a Tuition Reset Right for Your School?
Lucie Lapovsky, NAIS:
https://www.nais.org/articles/pages/member/reimagine-tuition_is-a-tuition-reset-right-for-your-school.pdf

Reimagine Tuition: Three Considerations for Independent School Tuition Setting, Lucie Lapovsky, NAIS:
https://www.nais.org/getmedia/18421e95-8cdf-4f11-af62-432866884f75/Reimagine-Tuition_Considerations-for-Tuition-Setting.pdf

ENDNOTES

[1] NAIS, "Reopening and Tuition Plans for 2020-2021," NAIS Snapshot, Week of July 27, 2020; online at https://www.nais.org/getmedia/15d5b8f8-32ed-44e0-8422-1a23ca13ca0f/NAISsnapshotSurveyTuition073120.pdf.

[2] Jefferson Burnett and Ioanna Wheeler, "NAIS Advisory: The International Student Landscape," NAIS, May 2020; online at https://www.nais.org/articles/pages/member/global/nais-advisory-the-international-student-landscape/.

[3] NAIS, "Financial Aid," NAIS Snapshot, Week of May 11, 2020; online at https://www.nais.org/getmedia/522687d7-0ef5-449a-9da7-a0c3c34ad400/NAISsnapshotSurvey051520FinAid.pdf.

[4] NAIS, "Admissions," NAIS Snapshot, Week of March 29, 2021; online at https://www.nais.org/getmedia/918ebe00-d6d2-4a5e-a51d-ea94a56d181a/

NAISsnapshotSurvey040221admissions.pdf.

[5] Mark J. Mitchell, "The Affordability Outlook," *2020-2021 NAIS Trendbook* (Washington, DC: NAIS, 2020), p. 54.

[6] U.S. Bureau of Economic Analysis, Employment Data; online at https://www.bea.gov/data/employment/employment-by-industry.

[7] Financial aid data from School and Student Services (SSS).

[8] Doug Lederman, "Aid Application Data Portend Dip in Low-Income, Minority Students," *Inside Higher Ed*, February 16, 2021; online at https://www.insidehighered.com/admissions/article/2021/02/16/data-financial-aid-applications-portend-drop-low-income-minority#:~:text=Aid%20Application%20Data%20Portend%20Dip,disadvantaged%20backgrounds%20seem%20disproportionately%20affected.

[9] EdChoice, "October 2020 General Population Polling Presentation," slides 17-19; online at https://docplayer.net/199411476-Edchoice-october-2020-gen-pop-national-polling-presentation.html.

[10] Ibid.

[11] Ibid.

[12] NAIS, "Admissions," NAIS Snapshot, Week of January 11, 2021; online at https://www.nais.org/getmedia/7aa8ef55-8cf0-49a7-8e93-25014d0131d2/NAISsnapshot011521admissions.pdf.

The
PHILANTHROPY
Outlook

By Davis Taske and Karla Taylor

Davis Taske is a research associate at NAIS.

Karla Taylor is co-editor of the *Trendbook*.

TRENDING
FOR 2021-2022

- Annual funds and capital campaigns grew at most independent schools despite the pandemic.

- Online giving is increasing substantially, and advancement officers express continued openness to a blend of virtual and in-person fundraising activities in the future.

- Schools face an opportunity to expand their donor pool by retaining new pandemic-era donors.

Τ he big question facing fundraisers in 2020 was simple: Will the pandemic hurt fundraising results? For the majority of nonprofits, including independent schools, the answer was a reassuring *no*.

Released in June 2021, the annual *Giving USA* report was a source of bright spots from a dark time. In calendar year 2020, overall charitable giving in the United States was up 5.1% over 2019, for a record $471.44 billion in current dollars. Giving to education grew by 9.0% to $71.34 billion. The *Giving USA* report called this "substantial growth in any year and somewhat remarkable in such a tumultuous one."[1]

Despite the pandemic, "The factors that we know impact giving continue to impact giving," said Anna Pruitt, the report's managing editor. "The health of the stock market and the state of the economy, legislation and tax policy, and unforeseen events and circumstances—all of those things continue to impact charitable giving. The stronger economy is the thing that's really lifting giving."[2]

A large number of NAIS members experienced that giving lift in both annual funds and capital campaigns.

Just as the rest of the world was driven to do more online during the pandemic, so were donors. A record number made their gifts electronically and, to a greater degree than ever before, via their mobile devices.

And although smaller groups of major donors have accounted for a larger share of gifts in the past, some schools may have opportunities to broaden their donor pool by retaining new pandemic-era donors.

Despite Fears About the Impact of COVID-19 on Donations, Most Independent Schools' Annual Funds and Capital Campaigns Fared Well in 2020-2021*

Facing an unpredictable future when the pandemic hit in early 2020, many independent school advancement staffs felt forced to reconsider business as usual and

---

* Percentages in the figures in this chapter may not equal 100% due to rounding.

then lower expectations accordingly. Among respondents to a September 2020 NAIS Snapshot Survey, 47% had decreased their total fundraising goals compared to the previous fiscal year. Only 17% had increased their goals (Figure 1).[3]

However, by spring 2021, actual results had alleviated those fears for many schools—raising hopes that the pandemic wouldn't cause lasting damage to future fundraising.

According to a May 2021 NAIS Snapshot Survey about annual fund results, 66% of respondents reported raising more than they had in 2019-2020. In fact, 30% reported that their annual fund giving increased by 11% or more.[4]

Concerned about pursuing capital gifts amid the pandemic, 16% of respondents to the September 2020 Snapshot Survey reported pausing their capital campaigns.[5] But many schools continued their campaigns and reaped the rewards. In the May 2021 Snapshot Survey, nearly half of respondents (49%) reported that their capital campaigns raised more than they had in 2019-2020 (Figure 2).[6]

FIGURE 1: **Change in Fundraising Goals and Results, 2020-2021 vs. 2019-2020**

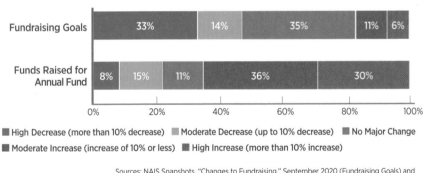

Sources: NAIS Snapshots, "Changes to Fundraising," September 2020 (Fundraising Goals) and "Advancement," May 2021 (Funds Raised)

FIGURE 2: **Change in Capital Campaign Fundraising, 2020-2021 vs. 2019-2020**

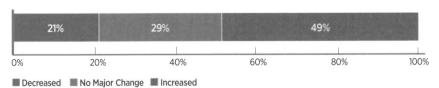

Source: NAIS Snapshot, "Advancement," May 2021

That's an improvement from prospects just three months earlier: In a February 2021 NAIS Snapshot Survey, only 35% of respondents said they had raised more than they had in 2019-2020.[7] This mirrors a trend in the nonprofit world at large, in which optimism about giving rose as COVID-19 vaccines emerged along with hopes for a better future.

What explains the better-than-expected fundraising results? Three factors played a part.

The stock market. Usually when the U.S. economy contracts, markets plunge and giving drops, as was the case in the Great Recession of 2007-2009.[8] Not this time. The S&P 500 hit a pandemic low of 2,237.40 in March 2020 but recovered and just kept rising. It closed at 4,395.26 on July 30, 2021—a 96.4% increase.[9]

Bequests. According to *Giving USA*, bequests accounted for 9% of all gifts in 2020 and increased 10.3% over 2019, to an estimated $41.91 billion. The main drivers of this increase: shifting generational demographics as baby boomers age and the general upswing of interest in planned giving that some nonprofits have reported during the pandemic.[10]

Targeted messaging. Asked what worked well for their fundraising campaigns during the pandemic, respondents to the February 2021 Snapshot Survey cited the desire of donors—especially those with the capacity to give more—to help in any way they could. Among the themes schools highlighted were a greater need for financial aid for families affected by COVID-19, the challenge to make up for lost revenue, and the costs of reopening classrooms and programs safely.[11]

Online Fundraising Is Growing, and Virtual Events Are Likely to Supplement In-Person Activities in the Future

"What passes for normal life now happens almost entirely online," wrote Jason Abbruzzese, senior editor for NBC News Digital.[12] So it's not surprising that after a year when much of the world was stuck at home, more donors would want giving to be as easy as ordering groceries on a laptop or checking the news on a cellphone. It's also to be expected that advancement staffs would conceive of ways to blend the best of virtual and in-person engagement.

Online giving breaks records. According to the Blackbaud Institute, "2020 signified a tremendous amount of growth and maturity in online giving." Among the 4,964 nonprofits studied in Blackbaud's *Charitable Giving Report*:

- 12.9% of total fundraising came from online giving, which made 2020 the

FIGURE 3: **Percentage of Total Funds Raised in K-12 Schools via Online Giving, 2014 to 2020**

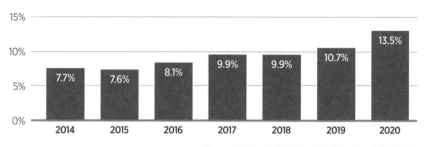

Sources: Blackbaud Institute, *Charitable Giving Reports*, 2014-2020

first year when more than 10% of funds raised came via online sources. Among K-12 institutions in this study, the share was 13.5% (Figure 3).

- Online giving in 2020 grew 20.7% year over year.
- Among online donations in 2020, "an estimated 28% … were made using mobile devices. This has grown steadily since 2014, when it was just 9% of online donations" (Figure 4).[13]

NAIS's May 2021 Snapshot Survey measured the percentage of donations that

FIGURE 4: **Percentage of Overall Online Donations Made with a Mobile Device, 2014 to 2020**

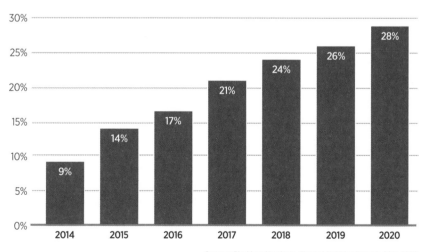

Sources: Blackbaud Institute, *Charitable Giving Reports*, 2014-2020

occurred online (rather than percentage of funds raised, as with the Blackbaud report). Respondents to NAIS's survey also reported strong interest in online giving: 58% said that at least half their donations come via online giving.[14]

Hybrid and virtual activities may be here to stay. Giving isn't the only thing that has moved online. After the start of the pandemic in early 2020, many NAIS members went virtual with activities that they had previously assumed could be conducted only in person. As of September 2020, 59% of independent schools had implemented new fundraising events, primarily virtual and socially distanced outdoor events.[15]

After trying the online experience, many schools report being open to hybrid approaches in the future. Among respondents to the May 2021 Snapshot Survey:

- 76% said alumni events will be both in person and virtual moving forward.
- 74% said one-on-one major donor solicitation will be in person and virtual.
- 80% said one-on-one major donor stewardship will be in person and virtual.[16]

Exactly how these intentions will play out in post-pandemic times is hard to predict. Among respondents to the NAIS Snapshot Survey, no more than 4% said they would choose virtual-only options for alumni events, donor solicitation, or stewardship.[17] And the very human desire to mix and mingle may ultimately dictate the return to in-person options for events such as galas.

Nevertheless, fundraisers now have firsthand experience with ways in which online events can cost less while enabling people all over the world to participate. This suggests that advancement staffs may continue to use hybrid engagement activities in creative ways.

Although Major Gifts Continue to Dominate, the Pandemic May Have Brought in Donors Who Can Expand the Future Pool

Major donors are vital to successful independent school advancement programs, and many schools reported that these donors continued to give generously during the pandemic. According to NAIS's May 2021 Snapshot Survey, 60% of respondents raised more funds from major donors in 2020-2021 than the year before (Figure 5).[18]

In addition, 55% of respondents to the May 2021 Snapshot survey reported

FIGURE 5: Amount Raised from Major Donors to Independent Schools, 2020-2021 vs. 2019-2020

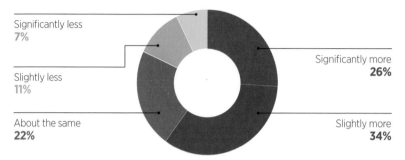

Significantly less
7%

Slightly less
11%

About the same
22%

Significantly more
26%

Slightly more
34%

Source: NAIS Snapshot, "Advancement," May 2021

that gifts from major donors were a greater share of total funds raised than in the year before (Figure 6).[19] Giving became more concentrated even though schools maintained their broad outreach to donors. Despite some qualms about soliciting during the pandemic, only 3% of survey respondents reported limiting the number of people they solicited, according to the September 2020 NAIS Snapshot.[20]

Generous current support from top donors is good news. But like all non-profits, independent schools face the challenge of maintaining a pipeline of gifts of all sizes to bring in donors for tomorrow. A different pandemic-era trend could offer schools the opportunity to expand and balance their donor pools.

The number of donors across all philanthropic giving in the United States

FIGURE 6: Change in Total Funds Raised from Major Donors in 2020-2021 Compared to Previous Years

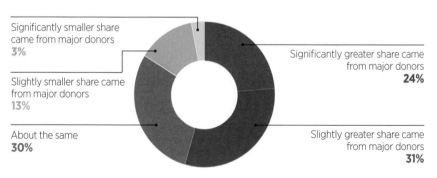

Significantly smaller share
came from major donors
3%

Slightly smaller share came
from major donors
13%

About the same
30%

Significantly greater share came
from major donors
24%

Slightly greater share came
from major donors
31%

Source: NAIS Snapshot, "Advancement," May 2021

increased 10% in the first quarter of 2021 compared to the first quarter of 2020, according to the Fundraising Effectiveness Project's *2021 First Quarter Fundraising Report*.[21] This increase is "finally reversing a decade-long trend of fewer U.S. households donating money," wrote Jon Biedermann, chair of the Fundraising Effectiveness Project. "And donor retention, too, is up, which foretells increasing revenue in the future."[22] By the end of the first quarter of 2021, the Fundraising Effectiveness Project reported that nonprofits had retained 13.6% more donors from 2020 than they had between 2019 and 2020.[23]

Philanthropy-watchers speculate that 2020-2021 created a giving moment—a time of shared community and deeply felt urgency. People cared about the problems brought on by COVID-19 and the issues raised in the racial justice movement. As a result, they felt moved to contribute to the solutions through giving. In education, donors could see that their giving would have a direct impact on schools' ability to reopen safely. Wanting to be part of the moment prompted some independent schools to use the targeted messaging that contributed to increased annual and capital giving in 2020-2021—and helped schools avoid fundraising disaster.

Philanthropy-watchers also know that moments don't last forever. The prediction below comes from a GivingTuesday Data Commons report called *Giving in Unprecedented Times: A Lookback at 2020 U.S. Giving Data and Trends*.

> Charitable giving patterns will return to pre-2020 trends. We expect fewer and weaker giving moments to drive fundraising. We anticipate this may result in a decrease in [year-over-year] revenue, huge retention drops for human services, and a spike in recapture rates for other causes.[24]

The report speculates that for many nonprofits, an increased focus on recapturing donors can counteract lapsed giving and the shrinking donor base. The report notes, "As fundraising returns to pre-2020 levels, there will be a larger-than-ever pool of recently lapsed (and likely highly engaged) donors."[25] Many independent schools now know that the pandemic didn't damage their fundraising. So the big question becomes, how can schools pivot to keep donors' interest high and sustain—or increase—their level of giving?

Strategic Questions

How have your annual fund and capital giving changed since the pandemic started? How do you expect them to change over the short and long term?

What does your school do now to attract bequests and other types of planned giving? What could it do better?

How can you target your messages to meet changing circumstances and to appeal to different stakeholder groups?

Given the growing importance of online giving, how could your website be more effective as a fundraising tool? What could you do to enable quick and convenient mobile giving?

Going forward, which activities would work best in virtual or hybrid formats? Which should go back to being in-person activities? How can you capitalize on the best of both?

What can you do to diversify the pool of stakeholders you reach out to? How can you retain new donors from the giving moment that the pandemic has presented? How well do you use the right giving channels with the right stakeholder groups to maximize giving?

Action Steps

Use NAIS's Data and Analysis for School Leadership (DASL) to evaluate your annual giving numbers before, during, and after the pandemic. Examine how your school's giving compares to that of other schools in your area, especially schools that have similar enrollments or tuition levels. Explore how your giving amounts and participation rates vary by stakeholder group and see whether there are any groups that can be better engaged.

Also use DASL to benchmark your capital campaign before and after the pandemic. Compare your median capital giving by donor segment to giving at peer schools.

Review NAIS's Jobs-to-Be-Done research on why donors give to independent schools. Evaluate what "Jobs" your donors want your school to do for them, and target your messaging to these goals and desired outcomes.

Conduct a thorough audit of the donation areas of your website. Examine everything from the landing page to page-completion rates. Compare the experiences on desktop computers, tablets, and mobile devices. Test your strategies to increase the number of visitors who complete the gift after arriving at your donation page.

Make it a priority to better organize your advancement program to raise the largest possible gifts now without neglecting those who give smaller gifts or younger donors who will make up your pipeline in the future.

 ## Resources

Charitable Giving Report: Using 2020 Data to Transform Your Strategy, **Blackbaud Institute:**
https://institute.blackbaud.com/charitable-giving-report/

Fundraising Effectiveness Project:
http://afpfep.org/reports/

Gifts That Give Back, **Karla Taylor, NAIS:**
https://my.nais.org/s/store#/store/browse/detail/a133m000008HymEAAS

Giving USA:
https://givingusa.org/

Handbook of Philanthropy at Independent Schools,
Helen Colson (ed.), NAIS:
https://my.nais.org/s/store#/store/browse/detail/a133m000008HyINAAS

"Jobs-to-Be-Done Study on Independent School Donors," NAIS:
https://www.nais.org/articles/pages/research/nais-research-jobs-to-be-done-study-on-independent-schools-donors/

NAIS Data and Analysis for School Leadership (DASL):
https://dasl.nais.org/

The NAIS Planned Giving Primer, **Helen A. Colson, NAIS:**
https://www.nais.org/articles/pages/member/nais-planned-giving-primer/

The Trustee's Role in Fundraising: A Pain-Free Guide to Making a Major Difference for Your School, **Karla Taylor, NAIS:**
https://my.nais.org/s/store#/store/browse/detail/a133m000007XhPBAA0

ENDNOTES

[1] *Giving USA 2021: The Annual Report on Philanthropy for the Year 2020*, a publication of Giving USA Foundation, 2021, researched and written by the Indiana University Lilly Family School of Philanthropy, p. 11; online at www.givingusa.org.

[2] Eden Stiffman and Michael Theis, "Giving Grew in a Tumultuous Year But Not for All. What's Ahead in 2021?" *The Chronicle of Philanthropy*, June 15, 2021; online at https://www.philanthropy.com/article/giving-grew-in-a-tumultuous-year-but-not-for-all-whats-ahead-in-2021.

[3] NAIS, "Changes to Fundraising," NAIS Snapshot, Week of September 7, 2020; online at https://www.nais.org/getmedia/3b257ee2-63e8-46e4-9f15-70b92c894bb3/NAISsnapshotSurvey091120fundraising.pdf.

[4] NAIS, "Advancement," NAIS Snapshot, Week of May 3, 2021; online at https://www.nais.org/getmedia/caf72d12-a472-41de-83be-1c7860f973f6/NAISsnapshotSurveyAdvancement050721.pdf.

[5] NAIS, "Changes to Fundraising," September 2020.

[6] Ibid.

[7] NAIS, "Advancement," NAIS Snapshot, Week of February 1, 2021; online at https://www.nais.org/getmedia/512d8ed6-8a7c-4976-a9bc-e049f4e43867/NAISsnapshotSurvey020521.pdf.

[8] Stiffman and Theis, "Giving Grew in a Tumultuous Year."

[9] Investopedia Team, "What Is the History of the S&P 500?" April 5, 2021; online at https://www.investopedia.com/ask/answers/041015/what-history-sp-500.asp. S&P Dow Jones Indices, S&P 500®; online at https://www.spglobal.com/spdji/en/indices/equity/sp-500/#overview.

[10] Stiffman and Theis, "Giving Grew in a Tumultuous Year."

[11] NAIS, "Advancement," February 2021.

[12] Jason Abbruzzese, David Ingram, and Sawyer Click, "The Coronavirus Pandemic Drove Life Online. It May Never Return," NBC News, March 28, 2020; online at https://www.nbcnews.com/tech/internet/coronavirus-pandemic-drove-life-online-it-may-never-return-n1169956.

[13] Blackbaud Institute, "Online Giving Trends," in *Charitable Giving Report: Using 2020 Data to Transform Your Strategy* (Charleston, SC: 2021); online at https://institute.blackbaud.com/charitable-giving-report/online-giving-trends/.

[14] NAIS, "Advancement," May 2021.

[15] NAIS, "Changes to Fundraising," September 2020.

[16] NAIS, "Advancement," May 2021.

[17] Ibid.

[18] Ibid.

[19] Ibid.

[20] NAIS, "Changes to Fundraising," September 2020.

[21] *The NonProfit Times*, "Study: First Quarter 2021 Fundraising Beat 2020," June 22, 2021; online at https://www.thenonprofittimes.com/donors/study-first-quarter-2021-fundraising-beat-2020/.

[22] Jon Biedermann, "Breaking News: Americans Give More Generously and More People

Give—But Not All Nonprofits Benefit," Fundraising Effectiveness Project, June 23, 2021; online at https://afpglobal.org/FundraisingEffectivenessProject.

[23] *The NonProfit Times,* "Study: First Quarter 2021."

[24] GivingTuesday Data Commons, *Giving in Unprecedented Times: A Lookback at 2020 U.S. Giving Data and Trends* (2021); online at https://www.givingtuesday.org/wp-content/uploads/2021/05/GT_2020LookBack_Report-FINAL.pdf.

[25] Ibid.

The
GOVERNANCE
AND LEADERSHIP
Outlook

By Anne-Marie Balzano and Margaret Anne Rowe

Anne-Marie Balzano
was director of governance
and leadership at NAIS
until April 2021.

Margaret Anne Rowe
is a research analyst
at NAIS.

TRENDING
FOR 2021-2022

- The head-board partnership remained strong during the pandemic.

- Head of school stress and burnout were exacerbated by the crisis.

- Head turnover remained flat in 2020, but major shifts are expected.

The pandemic altered the very fabric of the independent school landscape, pushing heads and boards to adopt new governance and leadership practices. During the pandemic, many schools focused on short-term objectives to address the daily challenges brought on by the crisis. Most heads agreed that their boards worked collaboratively and supported their health and well-being. However, heads also said that their boards struggled to understand their role in the crisis and to create long-term goals to address their school's sustainability.

As might be expected, the ongoing nature of the pandemic increased the amount of stress heads of school felt in their leadership role. Prior NAIS research has highlighted heads' struggles with work-life balance and feelings of isolation, but the pandemic ushered in two new stressors: unpredictability and community polarization.[1]

How will the pandemic affect head of school tenure and turnover? Data show a decline in head of school turnover during the pandemic. This could be due to boards' unwillingness to engage in a leadership transition or heads' hesitation to engage in a job search during the crisis. However, NAIS research suggests that some heads are planning to leave their current positions within the next few years.[2]

Heads Rated Their Boards Highly During the First Year of the Pandemic, Particularly on Short-Term Priorities

As NAIS's online *Trustees' Guide* notes, one of the most important jobs of an independent school's board of trustees is to support the head of school. As partners, head and board articulate the school's mission and vision; create, review, and evaluate the school's plans on an ongoing basis; and present a united front to stakeholders.[3] Dysfunction within this partnership impedes both parties' effectiveness and puts the organization at risk for problems ranging from strategic misalignment to toxic culture. It can also lead to an untimely head departure.

In April 2020, when NAIS surveyed heads of school regarding their boards' performance of typical governance duties during the pandemic, most trustees received high marks. On average, boards received scores above 4 (on a 1 to 5 scale) on shorter-term priorities, such as supporting and collaborating with the head of school and engaging in appropriate decision-making. However, heads rated their boards less highly on performance metrics such as board members' understanding of their responsibilities during a crisis and the board's ability to establish shared goals and metrics with the head of school.[4]

In April 2021, heads reported similar perceptions of their boards' performance. More heads gave their boards higher scores on important performance metrics than in 2020: 76% of boards were rated 4 or 5 on their understanding of their responsibilities in a crisis (65% in 2020), while 64% received a 4 or 5 on establishing mutual goals and success metrics with the head (57% in 2020). However, slightly fewer heads felt that their boards were supportive—a decline from 83% in 2020 to 79% in 2021 (Figure 1).[5]

FIGURE 1: Percent of Heads Rating Their Board's Performance Highly* in Typical Areas of the Head-Board Relationship, 2020 and 2021

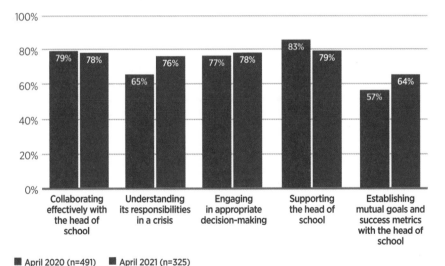

■ April 2020 (n=491) ■ April 2021 (n=325)

* Rated 4 or 5 on a 1 to 5 scale where 5 equals "extremely well"

Sources: NAIS Snapshots, "The Board/Head Relationship," April 2020, and "Leadership, Governance, and DEI," March 2021

The strength of the head-board partnership has a profound impact on the head's ability to effectively navigate not only a crisis but also the daily demands of the leadership role.

Heads Report Increased Stress

For heads of school, the pandemic didn't just compound the challenge of maintaining a collaborative relationship with the board of trustees. It also amplified the stress heads feel even in normal times.

In a comparison of interview data from early 2020 with survey data from October 2020 and head of school reflections from March 2021, three key themes emerge: Heads are stressed because of poor work-life balance, feelings of isolation in their role, and the sheer complexity of the headship job.[6] Already identified as one of the five biggest challenges in the head-board relationship, increased head of school stress makes it difficult to address the other challenges.[7]

Although all of the stressors of normal, pre-pandemic life remained, two new forms of stress emerged. When asked about the most stressful or challenging aspects of headship, 35% of respondents to the October 2020 NAIS Snapshot Survey named "unknowns/constant change," while 41% mentioned their "divided, difficult community."[8] Unpredictability, difficulty in planning, and fear due to COVID-19 were elements of "constant change" that heads described frequently in the March 2021 reflections. They also described communities divided about school reopening decisions as well as racial reckoning and polarizing U.S. politics (Table 1).[9]

A long-term struggle for heads has been how to balance work with self-care. In October 2020, 53% of heads mentioned that maintaining personal health and well-being was the most difficult or challenging aspect of their role.[10] By April 2021, 60% were dissatisfied with the time they had for family and friends and 64% with the time they had for themselves. Fifty-five percent were dissatisfied with the amount of time they had to spend on pandemic-related tasks (Figure 2). Although 73% of heads believed that their job was worth the stress, this was a *decrease* of 13 percentage points from 2009.[11]

Heads Stayed in Their Jobs in 2020, But More Transitions Loom

Despite the pandemic, the overall rate of school leadership transitions was on par with recent years. In 2020-2021, just 11% of NAIS schools reported a new head of school, down slightly from 12% in 2019-2020. However, it's interesting to take

TABLE 1: **Heads' Descriptions of Major Stressors Before and During the Pandemic***

	January-Early March 2020	Early October 2020	Early March 2021
Work-life balance	"There's no off switch.... It's 24/7/365 in a way that's different than even two years ago."	"Personally, this is taking a toll.... I am questioning whether it's worth it."	"I feel overloaded with too much information and not enough black and white, clear direction....
Feelings of isolation	"There are a lot of things that I don't—I can't—talk to anybody else about."	"It's hard to stay strong for others when we are the only one who can fully see the complete picture."	"I get into very dark places not knowing who to trust, and I also constantly worry about how I am being judged.... The hardest part is that the normal stresses of a headship—student/ family issues, faculty/ staff issues, board issues, etc.—are absolutely magnified by 1000, and I have very little emotional or psychological room."
Complexity of the job	"There's this constant realignment of focus... and you can make that shift a dozen or more times in a day."	"Everything we are doing this year is more difficult and time-consuming. Even the most mundane tasks... have now become quite challenging and tedious."	
Lack of predictability		"Decisions and the scenarios/people/ needs affecting those decisions can change on a dime. Flexibility is one thing—chaos is more how this year feels."	
Community polarization		"Everyone believes their truth is the truth, even though their desires/opinions in many cases are unknowingly at direct odds with other community members."	"A percentage of my faculty will feel I have thrown them to the wolves [for a quarantine-related decision].... The parents will largely support the decision, but a percentage will email that it's not doing enough to support their students [or] working parents."

*Quotes are based on a sampling of interviews conducted by NAIS and personal reflections submitted by school leaders.

Sources: Margaret Anne Rowe, "Head Turnover at Independent Schools, Part II: Supporting School Leadership," NAIS; Davis Taske, unpublished analysis of NAIS Snapshot, "Adult Health and Well-Being," October 2020; and data collected by Melinda Tsapatsaris, personal communication

FIGURE 2: **Head Satisfaction, 2021***

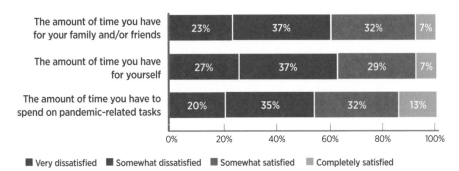

■ Very dissatisfied   ■ Somewhat dissatisfied   ■ Somewhat satisfied   ■ Completely satisfied

Totals do not equal 100 due to rounding. n=579

Source: Margaret Anne Rowe, *The State of Independent School Leadership 2021*, NAIS

a closer look at unexpected turnover, which NAIS defines as any termination or nonrenewal of a head in place for three years or fewer. Unexpected turnover rose somewhat over the past decade, from 15.9% of all headship transitions in 2012-2013 to 21.9% in 2019-2020. But during the pandemic, such turnover fell by 4.5 percentage points, decreasing to 17.4%.[12]

Recent independent school turnover mirrors higher education, where fewer presidents willingly stepped down during 2020 than in previous years. Similarly, however, the number was still within a normal range.[13]

FIGURE 3: **Heads' Future Plans, 2021**

LOOKING FORWARD, WOULD YOU SAY YOU PLAN TO TRANSITION FROM THIS HEADSHIP...

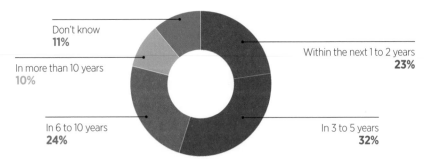

Source: Margaret Anne Rowe, *The State of Independent School Leadership 2021*, NAIS

In April 2021, when the pandemic school year was nearly over, 55% of heads reported that they intend to leave their current position within one to five years—higher than the 37% who said the same in 2009 during the Great Recession (Figure 3). That number was later reflected in 50% of schools reporting a head transition between 2010-2011 and 2014-2015. Still, subsequent turnover was not necessarily due to the crisis of the recession: Only 27% of heads in 2009 said they delayed their retirement because of the recession. Similarly, the COVID-19 crisis has convinced less than a quarter to change their timeline for leaving.[14] National data have shown that few workers change occupations during recessions.[15]

With headships in flux, the post-pandemic period will be a critical opportunity for boards and heads to examine their relationship. At schools, as at all non-profits, the nature of the head-board relationship directly influences the leader's degree of satisfaction. Additionally, leaders at schools with fewer head transitions were more likely to report that their board followed good governance practices.[16] Expectations of the head's duties may also differ between the two parties, often because of miscommunication during the hiring process.[17]

To help prevent discord, burnout, and head turnover following an exhausting period for school leaders, heads and boards will need to review and strengthen their communication and collaboration practices and proactively address the head's well-being.

 ## Strategic Questions

How might your board engage in more strategic conversations, both at the committee level and during full board meetings? What opportunities have emerged from the pandemic that the school might capitalize on in the future?

In what ways has your board provided support for your head of school during the pandemic? How might this support shift in the coming year to address stress factors such as isolation, work-life balance, and community polarization?

How does your board engage in authentic conversations around health and well-being for the head of school? The faculty and staff? Students? The school community?

What processes are in place for a leadership transition at your school?

Action Steps

Evaluate past board meeting agendas to determine how the board spends time during meetings. Make strategic and generative conversations a priority.

Examine your board's current structure to determine whether the right committees and task forces are in place to address post-pandemic opportunities and challenges.

Have the board meet with the head of school to determine which supports are most helpful and effective to address stress and nurture well-being.

Make time for reflection to address community polarization and the implications of the pandemic. What you do after a crisis is just as important as how you managed the crisis in the moment.

Ensure that the board has a formal process in place for head succession. Although a leadership transition may not be imminent, it is important to have a clearly articulated plan of action.

Resources

The Board Chair Handbook: An Essential Guide for Board Leaders at Independent Schools, John E. Creeden, NAIS:
https://my.nais.org/s/store#/store/browse/detail/a133m000008I0YDAA0

NAIS Leadership Through Partnership (LTP) Workshop:
https://www.nais.org/participate/institutes-workshops/leadership-through-partnership/

NAIS Principles of Good Practice for the Board of Trustees and *NAIS Principles of Good Practice for Independent School Trustees*:
https://www.nais.org/learn/principles-of-good-practice/

NAIS Trustees' Guide:
https://www.nais.org/trustees-guide/

Trustee Handbook, 10th Edition, Revised, Donna Orem and Debra P. Wilson, NAIS:
https://my.nais.org/s/store#/store/browse/detail/a133m000008HyIOAAS

The Trustee Table podcast, NAIS:
https://www.nais.org/learn/knowledge-center/governance-and-leadership/the-trustee-table/

What Are Boards Searching for When They Hire an Independent School Leader? NAIS:

https://www.nais.org/articles/pages/research/nais-jobs-to-be-done-research-what-are-boards-searching-for-when-hiring-a-head-of-school/

ENDNOTES

[1] NAIS, "The Board/Head Relationship," NAIS Snapshot, Week of April 13, 2020; online at https://www.nais.org/getmedia/a11745fd-c137-4a31-83e9-5c6c240b8021/NAISsnapshotSurvey041720.pdf. NAIS, "Leadership, Governance, and DEI," NAIS Snapshot, Week of March 29, 2021; online at https://www.nais.org/getmedia/060d7364-49d2-4b64-b61e-ff013fcdce30/NAISsnapshotSurvey040221DEI.pdf.

[2] Margaret Anne Rowe, *The State of Independent School Leadership 2021* (Washington, DC: NAIS, 2021); online at https://www.nais.org/articles/pages/research/nais-research-2021-state-of-independent-school-leadership-survey/.

[3] NAIS, "Section 7: Partner with the Head of School," *Trustees' Guide*; online at https://www.nais.org/trustees-guide/partner-with-the-head-of-school/.

[4] NAIS, "The Board/Head Relationship," April 2020.

[5] NAIS, "The Board/Head Relationship" and "Leadership, Governance, and DEI," March 2021.

[6] Davis Taske, unpublished analysis of NAIS Snapshot, "Adult Health and Well-Being," Week of October 5, 2020; online at https://www.nais.org/getmedia/5156c1f9-0ec7-4825-8e65-03127ae1f47f/NAIS_Snapshot-Survey_Adult-Health-Wellbeing_10-09-20.pdf. Margaret Anne Rowe, "Head Turnover at Independent Schools, Part II: Supporting School Leadership," NAIS, July 2021. Data collected by Melinda Tsapatsaris, personal communication.

[7] Margaret Anne Rowe, *Head Turnover at Independent Schools: Sustaining School Leadership* (Washington, DC: NAIS, February 2020); online at https://www.nais.org/articles/pages/research/nais-research-head-turnover-at-independent-schools-sustaining-school-leadership/.

[8] Taske, unpublished analysis.

[9] Taske, unpublished analysis. Tsapatsaris, personal communication.

[10] Taske, unpublished analysis.

[11] Rowe, *State of Independent School Leadership 2021*. NAIS, *The State of Independent School Leadership 2009: Report of Survey Research Among School Heads and Administrators* (Washington, DC: 2010); online at https://www.nais.org/Articles/Documents/Member/2009%20NAIS%20Leadership%20Report%20Final_web.pdf.

[12] NAIS, Data and Analysis for School Leadership (DASL), custom report.

[13] Eric Kelderman, "Is the Pandemic Pushing a Wave of Presidents Out? Not Yet," *The Chronicle of Higher Education*, November 24, 2020; online at https://www.chronicle.com/article/is-the-pandemic-pushing-a-wave-of-presidents-out-not-yet.

[14] Rowe, *State of Independent School Leadership 2021*. NAIS, *State of Independent School Leadership 2009*.

[15] Carlos Carrillo-Tudela, Bart Hobijn, and Ludo Visschers, "Career Changes Decline During Recessions," Federal Reserve Bank of San Francisco, *FRBSF Economic Letter*, March

31, 2014; online at https://www.frbsf.org/economic-research/files/el2014-09.pdf. Nick Bunker, "The State of Job Switching and Hiring," Indeed Hiring Lab, February 11, 2020; online at https://www.hiringlab.org/2020/02/11/job-switching-and-hiring/.

[16] BoardSource, *Leading with Intent: 2017 BoardSource Index of Nonprofit Board Practices* (Washington, DC: 2017); online at https://leadingwithintent.org/. Peter Horn, "Factors Affecting Head of School Tenure (FAHST) Study," data handout presented at the NAIS Annual Conference, February 2020.

[17] NAIS, "NAIS Jobs-to-Be-Done Research: What Are Boards Searching for When They Hire an Independent School Leader?"; online at https://www.nais.org/articles/pages/research/nais-jobs-to-be-done-research-what-are-boards-searching-for-when-hiring-a-head-of-school/.

The
WORKFORCE
Outlook

By Donna Orem

**Donna Orem is
president of NAIS.**

TRENDING
FOR 2021-2022

- The pandemic has reshaped the workforce, affecting K-12 education among other sectors.

- A new hybrid workforce is emerging in the wake of the pandemic.

- Well-being, collaboration, and professional development rate highly among employees' hopes for the post-pandemic workplace.

In recent years, the workforce has been constantly reshaping, influenced by changes in demographics, employee attitudes, the economic landscape, and other external forces. But rarely have these forces collided in the way they did in 2020 and 2021, when COVID-19 swept around the world. Schools and businesses shuttered overnight, and people retreated to their homes. Many people and organizations were left struggling financially.

Although the world will feel the pandemic's aftershocks for some time to come, the impact has already altered the workforce in significant ways. *Who* makes up the workforce is evolving as individuals lose jobs, retire, or consider switching professions. Job losses during the shutdown disproportionately impacted lower-income workers and those in service industries, including Black and Hispanic workers and women, and especially working mothers.[1]

Where people work is changing as well. The retreat from offices and classrooms early in the pandemic ushered in a new age of hybrid opportunities, making employees and employers alike aware of the benefits of remote work. And the stress and anxiety brought on by the twin pandemics of COVID-19 and racial injustice have changed employees' minds about *how* and *why* they work. Many are looking to their workplaces to support their well-being and create cultures with more opportunities for learning and collaboration.

The Pandemic Has Reshaped the Workforce

The makeup of the workforce has shifted dramatically as a result of a number of pandemic-related changes.

Whether because they left their jobs or their jobs left them, many workers have departed from the workforce. The pandemic has taken its toll on the American worker. According to the Pew Research Center, "From February 2020 to February 2021, a net 2.4 million women and 1.8 million men left the labor force ... representing drops of 3.1% and 2.1%, respectively." Pew researchers note that this is among the largest 12-month declines in the post-World War II era.[2]

Most of the job losses have been in the service sector, affecting Black and Hispanic workers more than any other groups. Early in the lockdown, the Economic Policy Institute reported that just one in six Hispanic workers was able to work remotely.[3] By March 2021, the Future Forum reported:

> Overall, Black unemployment (9.2%) far exceeds that of white unemployment (5.7%). Fewer than 1 in 5 Black employees are able to work from home. And 2 out of 5 Black small-business owners have gone out of business during the pandemic, twice the rate of white businesses.[4]

As more people were vaccinated and businesses reopened in the first half of 2021, some of these losses began to reverse. However, Pew researchers suggest that it could take "more than three years to recoup, assuming job creation proceeds at roughly the same monthly rate as it did from 2018 to 2019."[5]

More baby boomers have changed their minds about retirement. In 2018, the Pew Research Center found that most boomers were still in the workforce, and many of the oldest intended to stay. At that time, "29% of Boomers ages 65 to 72 were working or looking for work, outpacing the labor market engagement of the Silent Generation (21%) and the Greatest Generation (19%) when they were the same age."[6] In addition, according to a 2016 study conducted by the Employee Benefit Research Institute, "45% of workers ages 55 and older expected to retire *after* age 65, up from 15% of such workers in the 1996 survey."[7]

The pandemic altered that trajectory as attitudes changed and businesses shut down. In late 2020, approximately 28.6 million baby boomers left the workforce to retire. According to Pew researchers, "This is 3.2 million more Boomers than the 25.4 million who were retired in the same quarter of 2019."[8]

Some speculate that these retirements could drain leadership ranks, leaving organizations vulnerable. Others see it as the opportunity that Gen Xers and millennials need to advance in their careers.

Teachers have been shaken by their pandemic experiences, although the long-term effects are still uncertain. An October 2020 study conducted among government employees by the Center for State and Local Government Excellence highlighted the effects of the pandemic on public school teachers and other employees:

- Education employees' job satisfaction plummeted since the outset of the pandemic. General satisfaction fell from 69% in March 2020 to 44% in October 2020.

- Among K-12 employees, 38% said that working during the pandemic made them consider changing jobs. This compares to 25% of other government employees.
- Also among K-12 respondents, 60% reported that they and their family have been hurt financially by the pandemic, compared to 50% of other government employees.[9]

For independent schools, the market for great teachers may be more competitive for the foreseeable future. In a November 2020 NAIS survey of student and teacher wellness, 93% of the teachers who responded reported feeling overwhelmed "because my teaching workload seems endless."[10] In January 2021, 14% of independent schools responding to an NAIS Snapshot Survey noted more or significantly more midyear employee attrition than in previous years.[11]

In addition, 16% of the schools responding to the Snapshot Survey experienced teacher shortages, 16% saw more teachers retiring early, and 8% saw more teachers switching professions (Figure 1). At the same time, 37% of the schools reported that they were hiring more staff than pre-COVID levels.[12]

However, the situation began to change as vaccines became available for teachers. NAIS began to observe some positive signs in the NAIS Career

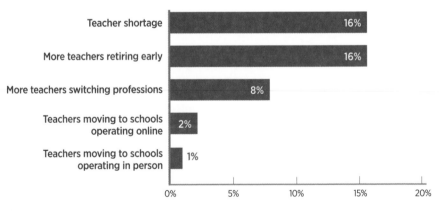

FIGURE 1: Teacher Hiring and Attrition at NAIS Schools, January 2021

IN YOUR SCHOOL, ARE YOU NOTICING ANY OF THE FOLLOWING TRENDS? SELECT ALL THAT APPLY.

Teacher shortage	16%
More teachers retiring early	16%
More teachers switching professions	8%
Teachers moving to schools operating online	2%
Teachers moving to schools operating in person	1%

Source: NAIS Snapshot, "Teacher Hiring and Attrition Rates," January 2021

Center. After the precipitous drop in job-seeker visits to the Career Center in spring 2020, visits rebounded in March 2021 and exceeded pre-COVID levels. By spring 2021, job postings to the Career Center were also exceeding pre-pandemic levels.[13]

Remote Work Births a New Hybrid Workforce

Just as the pandemic shaped *who* is in the workforce, it also shaped *where* individuals choose to work. According to a March 2021 Ipsos poll, 35% of employees expect some amount of workplace flexibility moving forward. Within that expectation are some particular wants and needs:

- 62% want to return to the office occasionally.
- 72% want some flexibility in the amount of time they spend in the office.
- 70% feel more productive when they have a flexible work schedule.
- 42% say that if their employer required them to return to the office full-time, they would look for another job with more flexibility.[14]

A McKinsey & Company study forecast that the shift to remote work will primarily benefit the highly skilled, highly educated sector of the workforce in a select group of industries, occupations, and geographies. To pinpoint that impact on specific professions, McKinsey examined two factors: (1) The maximum remote work potential—that is, all activities that theoretically could be performed remotely—and (2) the effectiveness of delivering that activity remotely.[15]

Using that lens, researchers found that the areas with the highest potential to succeed in a remote or hybrid setting were finance, insurance, management, business services, and information technology (Figure 2). They noted that many activities have "a clear benefit from being done in person." This is particularly so for teaching; they commented: "While teaching has moved to remote work during the pandemic, parents and teachers alike say that the quality has suffered."[16]

An earlier McKinsey study found that many employers were already moving to launch hybrid work options, with 38% saying that they expect their employees to work remotely two days per week and another 19% forecasting three or more days of remote work.[17] That could spell big shifts for urban economies, with significant impact on transportation, restaurants, and retail—where many of the lower-income jobs are.[18] The changes could also cause difficulties for organizations that traditionally operate face-to-face, like schools, when recruiting and

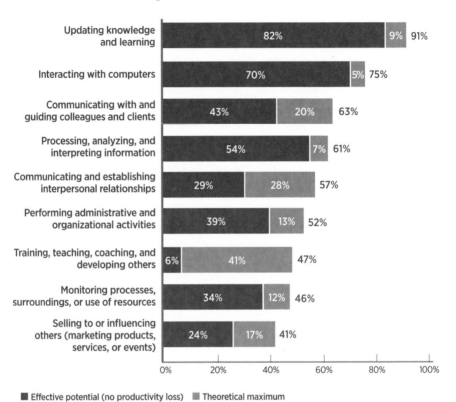

FIGURE 2: **Activities with the Highest Potential for Success in a Remote Setting**

Updating knowledge and learning: 82% / 9% — 91%
Interacting with computers: 70% / 5% — 75%
Communicating with and guiding colleagues and clients: 43% / 20% — 63%
Processing, analyzing, and interpreting information: 54% / 7% — 61%
Communicating and establishing interpersonal relationships: 29% / 28% — 57%
Performing administrative and organizational activities: 39% / 13% — 52%
Training, teaching, coaching, and developing others: 6% / 41% — 47%
Monitoring processes, surroundings, or use of resources: 34% / 12% — 46%
Selling to or influencing others (marketing products, services, or events): 24% / 17% — 41%

■ Effective potential (no productivity loss) ■ Theoretical maximum

Source: Exhibit from "What's next for remote work: An analysis of 2,000 tasks, 800 jobs, and nine countries," November 2020, McKinsey & Company, www.mckinsey.com. Copyright ©2021 McKinsey & Company. All rights reserved. Reprinted by permission.

retaining employees. School markets could also feel the impact if some employees go fully remote and choose to move to less expensive areas of the country, as happened during the period of widespread school closures (see Chapter 2, "The Demographic Outlook").

Any shift to remote work will have impacts—both positive and negative—on institutional culture, employee retention, and productivity. A *Harvard Business Review* report suggests that leaders assess remote work decisions through multiple lenses, such as (1) job and task suitability, (2) employee preferences, (3) projects and workflows, and (4) inclusion and fairness. When some workers are eligible to work remotely and others aren't, "feelings of unfairness in the workplace can hurt productivity, increase burnout, reduce collaboration and decrease retention."[19]

Employees Will Increasingly Value a Focus on Engagement, Well-Being, and Collaboration

How and *why* employees seek to work has also been altered by the pandemic, ushering in new challenges for school leaders as well as opportunities to rethink the school workforce. Several factors will drive the types of jobs the post-pandemic workforce seeks as well as how long employees stay in their jobs.

Engagement and well-being. Gallup describes engagement and well-being as reciprocal factors—each influences and adds on to the other. When engagement and well-being work together, "They are a super-charger for a thriving, productive workplace." However, the pandemic changed that relationship. For the first time since Gallup began researching these factors, engagement and well-being became disconnected.[20]

Employee engagement reached a record high at one point in 2020 and even ended the year one percentage point higher than 2019. Why? Gallup offers the following explanation:

> At a time when layoffs and furloughs abounded, employees were thankful to have jobs, experienced the benefits of increased flexibility and autonomy resulting from remote work, benefitted from strong leadership efforts to engage them, and rallied with coworkers to keep everything afloat. In short, employees were inspired by and united under a shared sense of purpose.[21]

Well-being, however, moved in the opposite direction. In April 2020, Americans' evaluations of their quality of life hit the lowest level since the Great Recession of 2007-2009. Only 46.5% described themselves as thriving, a 15% drop from the same time the previous year. Some improvement has occurred since then, but many people are still suffering from pandemic-induced stress, reverberations of social disconnection and social injustice, childcare strains, and uncertainty about the future. It's also notable that although engagement increased for remote workers, their levels of stress and worry also increased and continuously tracked higher than for in-person workers, reaching almost 20 percentage points higher in September 2020.[22]

How should employers interpret and act on these findings? Gallup suggests that they need to capitalize on the benefits that remote work can provide to employees while also monitoring them for changes in their well-being.[23]

Collaboration and professional development. The pandemic offers school leaders the opportunity to reexamine how teaching jobs are structured and to experiment with options that offer more time for collaboration and learning as a means to improve both student outcomes and teacher well-being. The National Center on Education and the Economy studied pre-pandemic data from a 2019 OECD survey on how teachers in top-performing public education systems around the world spent their time. The study found that teachers in the United States spent far more time teaching classes than their international counterparts, who devoted a larger share of their time to professional learning and collaboration activities. For example, teachers in Finland, Estonia, and Japan spent, on average, around 600 hours per year in classroom teaching compared to nearly 1,000 for U.S. teachers (Figure 3).[24]

Many independent schools already prioritize learning and collaboration for teachers. But the post-pandemic period offers a chance to pilot additional initiatives that could provide teachers with even more opportunities to improve their craft. The benefits could improve faculty recruitment and retention and, ultimately, drive improved student outcomes.

FIGURE 3: **Average Hours per Year Spent Teaching for Public School Teachers, by Country, 2019**

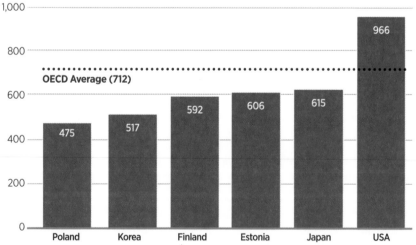

Source: Jennifer Craw, "Lesson Time: Reimagining Teachers' Working Hours," National Center on Education and the Economy; based on Organisation for Economic Co-operation and Development, *Education at a Glance 2020: OECD Indicators*

Strategic Questions

What steps can your school take to become an employer of choice, given the competitiveness of the emerging market for talent?

How could your school attract retired educators from the baby boom generation for contract or part-time work?

How can you leverage the opportunities that remote work provides without diminishing the advantages of in-person teaching for students and families?

How could you restructure the teaching week to give more time for professional learning and collaboration?

What policies and practices would you change if your school were designed around community well-being and belonging?

Action Steps

Probe NAIS's Jobs-to-Be-Done research for inspiration on ways to meet the workplace needs of your school's employees.

Interview employees to understand the benefits and constraints of their remote work experiences. Discuss how your school could replicate the benefits of the in-person experience or hybrid opportunities. Investigate how you could pilot hybrid work options, keeping in mind employee preferences, workflows, and fairness.

Conduct employee surveys to assess preferences and possibilities for remote work. Work with eligible employees to map out how work is done in the face-to-face environment and what potential obstacles could arise in a remote one.

If you choose to experiment with remote work for only a few roles, plan how you will respond to negative reactions from other staff members. Listen to staff wants and needs and involve them in the design process.[25]

Create a strategic succession plan for all key roles at your school and intentionally develop internal talent.

Survey faculty and staff routinely to understand their levels of engagement and well-being. Ensure that you're filtering the results to understand the differential impacts on various employee groups. Women and BIPOC employees, in particular, may be feeling more stress and disconnectedness during this time. Identify how you can best support these employees to enhance the well-being of all.

Consider offering training to supervisors so that they can identify and support faculty and staff who are in distress.

 **Resources**

"Future of Work," Deloitte:
https://www2.deloitte.com/us/en/insights/focus/technology-and-the-future-of-work.html?icid=top_technology-and-the-future-of-work

"Future of Work," McKinsey & Company:
https://www.mckinsey.com/featured-insights/future-of-work

"How COVID-19 Is Affecting Independent Schools," NAIS Snapshot Surveys:
https://www.nais.org/articles/pages/member/research/nais-snapshot-survey/

"Jobs-to-Be-Done Study on Independent School Teachers," NAIS:
https://www.nais.org/articles/pages/research/nais-research-jobs-to-be-done-study-on-independent-school-teachers/

"Lesson Time: Reimagining Teachers' Working Hours," Jennifer Craw, National Center on Education and the Economy:
https://ncee.org/2021/04/lesson-time-reimagining-teachers-working-hours/

Pew Research Center:
https://www.pewresearch.org/

Society for Human Resource Management:
https://www.shrm.org/

U.S. Bureau of Labor Statistics:
https://www.bls.gov/

"Workplace Insights," Gallup:
https://www.gallup.com/workplace/insights.aspx

ENDNOTES

[1] Rakesh Kochhar and Jesse Bennett, "US Labor Market Inches Back from the Covid-19 Shock, But Recovery Is Far from Complete," Pew Research Center, April 14, 2021; online at https://www.pewresearch.org/fact-tank/2021/04/14/u-s-labor-market-inches-back-from-the-covid-19-shock-but-recovery-is-far-from-complete/.

[2] Ibid.

[3] Elise Gould and Heidi Shierholz, "Not Everybody Can Work from Home: Black and Hispanic Workers Are Much Less Likely to Be Able to Telework," Economic Policy Institute, *Working Economics* Blog, March 19, 2020; online at https://www.epi.org/blog/black-and-hispanic-workers-are-much-less-likely-to-be-able-to-work-from-home/.

[4] Sheela Subramanian and Tina Gilbert, "A New Era of Workplace Inclusion: Moving from Retrofit to Redesign," Future Forum, March 11, 2021; online at https://futureforum.com/2021/03/11/dismantling-the-office-moving-from-retrofit-to-redesign/.

[5] Kochhar and Bennett, "US Labor Market Inches Back."

[6] Richard Fry, "Baby Boomers Are Staying in the Labor Force at Rates Not Seen in Generations for People Their Age," Pew Research Center, July 24, 2019; online at https://www.pewresearch.org/fact-tank/2019/07/24/baby-boomers-us-labor-force/.

[7] Employee Benefit Research Institute, "2016 RCS Fact Sheet #4: Age Comparisons Among Workers," Retirement Confidence Survey; online at https://www.ebri.org/docs/default-source/rcs/4_rcs_16-fs-4_age.pdf?sfvrsn=56e8302f_2.

[8] Richard Fry, "The Pace of Boomer Retirements Has Accelerated in the Past Year," Pew Research Center, November 9, 2020; online at https://www.pewresearch.org/fact-tank/2020/11/09/the-pace-of-boomer-retirements-has-accelerated-in-the-past-year/#:~:text=The%20job%20losses%20associated%20with,increased%20by%20about%20 1.1%20million.&text=In%20September%2C%2040%25%20of%20Boomers,up%20 from%2039%25%20in%20February.

[9] Rivka Liss-Levinson, *K-12 Public School Employee Views on Finances, Employment Outlook, and Safety Concerns Due to COVID-19* (Washington, DC: Center for State and Local Government Excellence at ICMA-RC, 2021); online at https://slge.org/assets/uploads/2021/02/2021-slge-cv19-k12-report.pdf.

[10] Carol Bernate, "Student and Teacher Wellness During the COVID-19 Pandemic," NAIS, November 2020; online at https://www.nais.org/articles/pages/research/nais-research-student-and-teacher-wellness-during-the-covid-19-pandemic/.

[11] NAIS, "Teacher Hiring and Attrition Rates," NAIS Snapshot, Week of January 11, 2021; online at https://www.nais.org/getmedia/927663e5-e878-4a6c-85a4-fd980beaa412/NAISsnapshot011521hiring.pdf.

[12] Ibid.

[13] NAIS, "A Look Back at the 2021 Hiring Season," NAIS Hiring Insights Series No. 9, June 5, 2021; online at https://www.youtube.com/playlist?list=PLzUTMyBEL6RYKgeALeH8JchPKrVxJqEUV.

[14] Ipsos, "Do Current Remote Workers Want to Return to the Office? It's Complicated," March 5, 2021; online at https://www.ipsos.com/en-us/news-polls/remote-workers-want-return-office.

[15] "What's Next for Remote Work: An Analysis of 2,000 Tasks, 800 Jobs, and Nine Countries," November 2020, McKinsey & Company, www.mckinsey.com.

[16] Ibid.

[17] Susan Lund et al., "What 800 Executives Envision for the Postpandemic Workforce," McKinsey & Company, September 23, 2020; online at https://www.mckinsey.com/featured-insights/future-of-work/what-800-executives-envision-for-the-postpandemic-workforce.

[18] "What's Next for Remote Work."

[19] Lynda Gratton, "How to Do Hybrid Right," *Harvard Business Review*, May-June 2021;

online at https://hbr.org/2021/05/how-to-do-hybrid-right?utm_medium=email&utm_source=newsletter_perissue&utm_campaign=bestofissue_activesubs_digital&deliveryName=DM128773.

[20] Ben Wigert et al., "The Wellbeing-Engagement Paradox of 2020," Gallup, March 13, 2021; online at https://www.gallup.com/workplace/336941/wellbeing-engagement-paradox-2020.aspx?utm.

[21] Ibid.

[22] Ibid.

[23] Ibid.

[24] Jennifer Craw, "Lesson Time: Reimagining Teachers' Working Hours," National Center on Education and the Economy, April 29, 2021; online at https://ncee.org/2021/04/lesson-time-reimagining-teachers-working-hours/.

[25] Gratton, "How to Do Hybrid Right."

The
EQUITY
AND JUSTICE
Outlook

By Caroline G. Blackwell and Amada Torres

Caroline G. Blackwell is
vice president for equity
and justice initiatives
at NAIS.

Amada Torres is
vice president of studies,
insights, and research.

TRENDING
FOR 2021-2022

- More women are becoming heads of independent schools, narrowing the representation gap, but people of color are still underrepresented.

- Salary gaps by gender are still present.

- Many independent schools made strides in diversity, equity, and inclusion work in 2020-2021, but some face controversies in related areas.

The past two decades tell a story of slow but steady progress for women and people of color in the highest reaches of independent schools. An examination of the data makes several points stand out. One of the most positive is that people of color and women of all races and ethnicities are serving as heads of independent schools in greater numbers than ever before.[*]

However, women heads still earn only 86 cents for every dollar their male counterparts earn. This salary gap is about the same as in 2010-2011. What's more, representation and pay for female heads are lower in independent schools than in public schools.[1]

In 2020 and 2021, progress in the head's office occurred against the backdrop of continued striving to increase racial equity in the United States in general and independent schools in particular. The Black@ movement was one impetus for many schools to act in support of diversity, equity, and inclusion (DEI).[2] But as this support grew in independent schools, conflicts surfaced when many state legislatures undertook efforts to oppose anti-racism activities in many areas of education.[3]

More Women and People of Color Have Become School Heads, But Large Gaps Remain by Race and Ethnicity

As of 2020-2021, 41% of independent school heads were women, compared to 33% in 2000-2001. This representation is the highest since NAIS started collecting data for this variable. During the same period, the number of heads of color increased from 3% to a record 10% (Figure 1).

Despite this good news, there is room for improvement.

The percentage of female heads is lower than that of female principals in public schools. As reported by the National Center for Education Statistics

---

[*] Unless otherwise noted, data in this chapter come from NAIS's Data and Analysis for School Leadership (DASL).

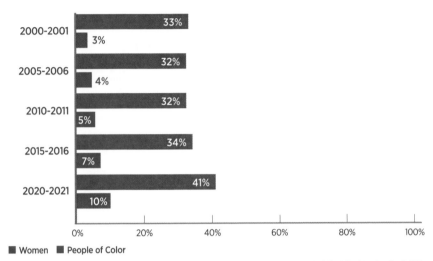

FIGURE 1: **Representation of Women and People of Color in Headship, 2000-2001 to 2020-2021**

■ Women ■ People of Color

Source: NAIS, Data and Analysis for School Leadership (DASL)

in 2017-2018, the latest numbers available, 54% of public school principals were women.[4]

The gender gap in independent school headship cannot be explained as a pipeline issue. In corporate America, the representation of women diminishes at every step of the leadership ladder.[5] But in independent schools, women are well-represented at the two levels preceding headship—teaching and adminis-

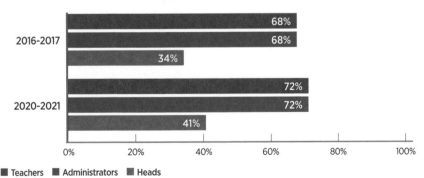

FIGURE 2: **Representation of Women in the Education Pipeline, 2016-2017 and 2020-2021**

■ Teachers ■ Administrators ■ Heads

Source: NAIS, Data and Analysis for School Leadership (DASL)

tration. Data from 2020-2021 show that 72% of both faculty and administrators were women. Similar levels of representation occurred a few years before, and yet, the gender gap at the headship level remained around 30 percentage points in both instances (Figure 2).

Women were not only present in large numbers among teachers and administrators. They were also a majority in several administrative leadership positions (except upper school heads) that are often considered precursors of headship (Figure 3).

Independent schools trail public schools in the share of heads of color. During the same period, from 2000-2001 to 2020-2021, the number of heads of color increased from 3% to 10% at independent schools. However, this percentage was still below the 22% of principals of color at public schools.[6] And, in contrast to the strong representation of women in various leadership roles in independent schools, people of color represented fewer than one in five in most of those roles, except for diversity practitioners, where they represented 84% of the total (Figure 3).

The representation of female heads and heads of color differed in schools of different sizes, grade levels, and locations. Smaller schools and elementary schools recorded higher numbers of female heads compared to larger schools and those serving students in high school (Figures 4 and 5). Similarly, there was a higher percentage of heads of color in smaller schools, especially in those with fewer than 101 students and elementary schools.

Also, larger percentages of female heads were found in the West (48%) and New England (42%). In particular, there were larger representations in individual states like Washington (53%), California (49%), and Connecticut (47%).

Even though the percentages are still small, schools in the West (16%) and in the Mid-Atlantic (11%) reported larger representations of heads of color. The largest percentage of heads of color (17%) was in California.

What reasons could account for gaps in the representation of female heads and heads of color in independent schools? An NAIS study, *People of Color and White Women in Independent School Headship*, provides two clues:

- Head search criteria tend to favor candidates from the academic side, while candidates from the operations and business side of the school are perceived as having less relevant experience. This bias disadvantages people of color and white women, who are more likely to come from nonacademic roles.

FIGURE 3: **Representation of Women and People of Color in Administrative Roles, 2020-2021**

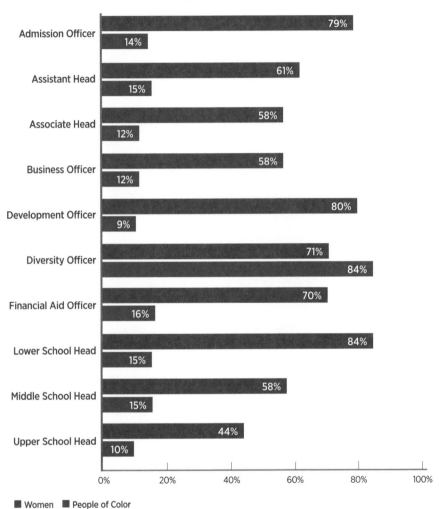

Source: NAIS, Data and Analysis for School Leadership (DASL)

- Female candidates, especially white women, were less likely than their male counterparts to have worked with a mentor or career sponsor. Many experts consider mentors crucial to achieving leadership goals.[7]

Salary Gaps by Gender Persist

As in other sectors, salary gaps by gender exist in independent schools. In 2020-2021, female heads earned 86 cents for every dollar their male counterparts earned—the same as in 2010-2011 (Figure 6). These gaps are not unique to inde-

FIGURE 4: Representation of Women and People of Color in Headship, by School Size, 2020-2021

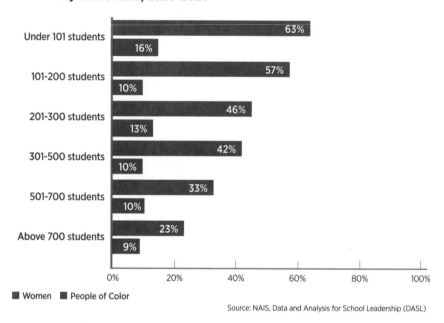

Source: NAIS, Data and Analysis for School Leadership (DASL)

FIGURE 5: Representation of Women and People of Color in Headship, by School Division, 2020-2021

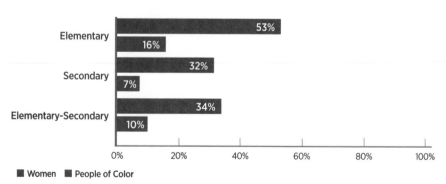

Source: NAIS, Data and Analysis for School Leadership (DASL)

FIGURE 6: **Median Head Salaries, by Gender, 2010-2011 and 2020-2021***

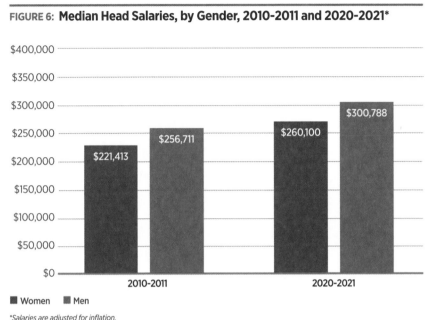

■ Women   ■ Men

*Salaries are adjusted for inflation.

Source: NAIS, Data and Analysis for School Leadership (DASL)

pendent schools. A recent study among public schools found that female principals make about $1,000 less a year on average than their male colleagues, a smaller gap than the one observed at independent schools. The same study notes that the gap persisted even when female principals were leading similar schools, had similar evaluations, and worked about the same number of hours as their male peers.[8]

One explanation of the salary gaps in independent schools is that the majority of female heads work in small schools or in elementary schools. Since these tend to offer smaller salaries for heads, female heads as a group earn less. Nonetheless, the data show that even when median salaries are compared by school size and grade level, salaries for female heads tend to be lower than for male heads.

Salary gaps by gender were larger among schools with fewer students. Although at schools with fewer than 201 students, median salaries for women were only slightly lower than those of male heads, the difference increases for schools with 201 to 300 students. Female heads in these schools earn 89 cents for each dollar earned by male heads. Only at schools with more than 500 students was the median salary for female heads on par with that of male heads. However, the gender gap was reversed at schools with 501 to 700 students. At these large schools, *men* earned 89 cents for every dollar that women earned (Figure 7).

FIGURE 7: **Median Head Salaries, by Gender and School Size, 2020-2021**

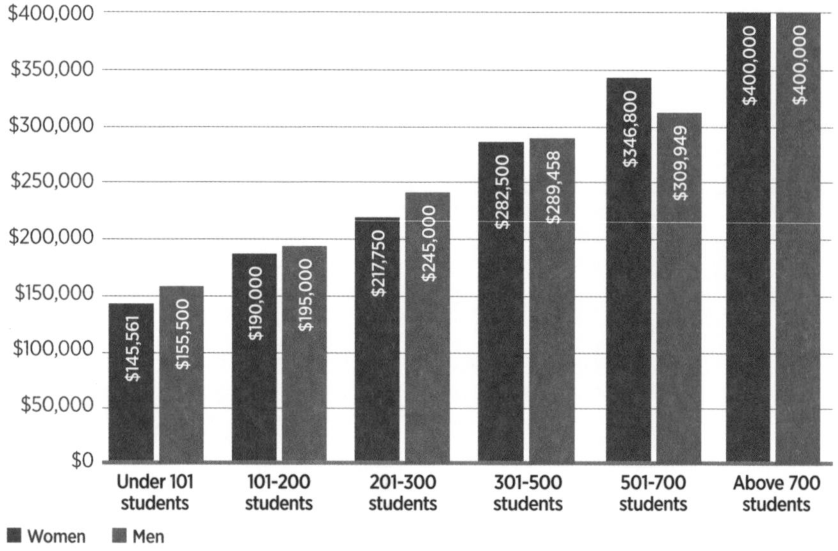

Women ■   Men ■

Source: NAIS, Data and Analysis for School Leadership (DASL)

Elementary schools also recorded larger salary gaps by gender. Gender gaps were observed when salaries are compared by grade level (Figure 8). The gaps were larger at elementary schools, where median salaries for women represented 85% of those for men. In secondary schools, the gap diminished, and in schools serving students in both elementary and secondary grades, female heads earn almost as much as their male colleagues.

The data also show changes in the salary gap based on race and ethnicity. In 2010-2011, heads of color earned 95 cents for every dollar earned by white heads, but by 2020-2021 that gap had disappeared. Heads of color earned slightly more than their white colleagues—$1.04 for every dollar white heads earned (Figure 9).

Other variables, like cost of living in the area where the school is located and total years of experience, may play a role in the determination of head salaries. But there are numerous instances where these additional factors don't justify the differences. To continue attracting a diverse and strong cadre of school leaders, boards must offer fair compensation to heads regardless of their demographic characteristics.

FIGURE 8: Median Head Salaries, by Gender and School Division, 2020-2021

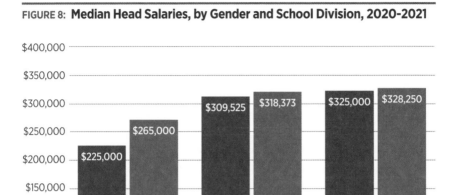

Source: NAIS, Data and Analysis for School Leadership (DASL)

FIGURE 9: Median Head Salaries, by Race and Ethnicity, 2010-2011 and 2020-2021*

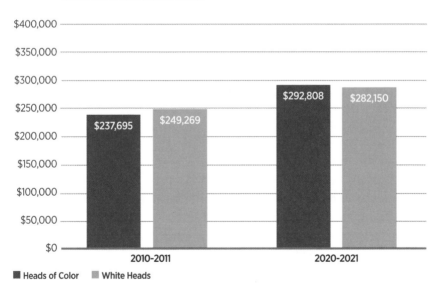

*Salaries are adjusted for inflation.

Source: NAIS, Data and Analysis for School Leadership (DASL)

Independent Schools Face Racial Reckoning and Pushback Against DEI Work in Some Places

In addition to trying to achieve gender and racial parity, independent schools continue to wrestle with other diversity, equity, and inclusion issues. Most notably, the murder of George Floyd by a Minneapolis police officer in May 2020 drew global attention to systemic racism, and it amplified calls for racial and social justice. Upwards of 23 million people in the U.S. protested after Floyd's murder,[9] as did thousands more in at least 60 other countries.[10]

For independent schools, the Black@ social media campaign, which gained renewed attention in the aftermath of the protests, revealed countless reports of pervasive historical and contemporary discrimination and anti-Black racism in school communities. In an NAIS Snapshot Survey from September 2020, 55% of schools reported that current and former students had shared their experiences of racism through the Black@ campaign. Half of the schools in the survey reported that current employees and former parents had shared stories about their schools, and 63% of schools said that former employees shared their experiences through the Black@ campaign.[11]

Large numbers of schools responded to these outpourings. In addition to making public statements (80%), more than half of the schools in the Snapshot Survey took meaningful steps, such as initiating anti-racism training for faculty and staff; pledging to adopt or adopting a multicultural curriculum; and convening Black students, alumni, or parents to engage in ongoing dialogue about the school climate. Half of the schools also pledged to increase the number of Black faculty (Figure 10).[12]

The calls for a racial reckoning that prompted businesses, nonprofit organizations, and schools to enact policies and programs to address systemic racism have generated backlash and an anti-anti-racism campaign.[13] Starting in early 2021, state legislatures across the country began banning teachers' use of words such as "racism" and "white supremacy" as well as "divisive concepts" related to sex and race.[14] This opposition centers around a legal analysis and practice known as Critical Race Theory (CRT). It was developed more than 40 years ago and is primarily taught in law schools to explain pervasive racial disparities in social and legal outcomes as the result of systemic policies and practices rather than as interpersonal animus.[15]

In response to widespread misinterpretation of CRT's tenets and purpose—in addition to unsubstantiated claims that the legal theory is widely taught in

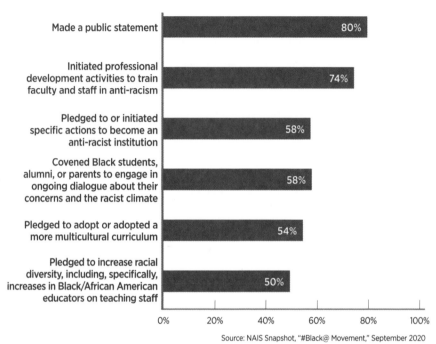

FIGURE 10: **Independent Schools' Responses to the Black@ Social Media Campaign, 2020**

Source: NAIS Snapshot, "#Black@ Movement," September 2020

schools—legislatures in more than 25 states (as of July 2021) had introduced bills or taken other steps to restrict how teachers in K-12 schools can discuss racism.[16] While such actions generally do not directly affect independent schools, they do speak to the political climate.

In times of crisis, programs and services that improve the experiences of individuals whose race, sexual orientation, gender identity, ability, and other identity statuses are marginalized may be put on hold as institutions address the crisis. One rationale is that crises require marshaling energy and resources to preserve what is perceived as fundamental or core. Although anecdotal evidence suggests that retrenchment has occurred in some areas during the pandemic, research shows that corporate and nonprofit leaders have continued to intensify their focus on board leadership related to DEI.[17]

A majority of independent schools have taken a step to hold themselves accountable to meaningful inclusion and anti-racist work by establishing a permanent committee to focus on diversity, equity, and inclusion work at the board level.

In an NAIS Snapshot Survey from March 2021, 31% of schools reported having such a board committee. Another 42% reported having a subcommittee, a task force, or other variation of these two.[18] This type of governance and leadership structure enables heads and boards to partner strategically to nurture a school climate and culture that values human differences and to allocate the means to ensure that those differences will be accepted and protected wholeheartedly.

 ## Strategic Questions

What process does your school follow when determining the head's salary and benefits? What considerations do you keep in mind when determining a fair compensation package?

How does the salary of your head of school compare to those of heads in similar schools based on size, grade levels offered, and location? What about benefits? What other considerations, such as cost of living, are included in determining compensation and benefits?

If your school is going through the process of hiring a new head, what steps in the process may be putting women and people of color at a disadvantage? How could you mitigate the impact that implicit bias may have on your hiring process? How might board members' experiences and expectations be hindering women and people of color from reaching headship?

How do you define diversity? Equity? Inclusion? Racial and social justice? What concepts, values, and principles inform your definitions?

How do you assess the progress of your DEI work? If you are not using data to drive your programming, how do you measure change and effectiveness?

Does your board have a standing DEI committee? If not, why not? If so, what (board-specific) DEI policies and practices has it created?

What have you learned about your school's climate and culture this year? Which students and families welcomed opportunities for on-site learning? Which groups felt more comfortable learning from home? What were the similarities and differences in these groups?

How confident and effective were you at managing conflict and tension in your school community? What will you do differently in the future?

When was the last review of your written policies related to DEI? Which policies might need updating? Are new policies needed?

Action Steps

When boards create head search committees, including individuals with diverse demographic and cultural backgrounds helps ensure a broad representation of viewpoints during the search process. Similarly, when selecting a search firm, search committees should inquire about the firm's methods, resources, and outreach efforts for recruiting a diverse array of candidates, including white women and people of color. Discuss the criteria used to select applicants, and set clear expectations and guidelines about the candidate pool you want to see, including diversity requirements.

Consider job requirements carefully. Assess whether the experience and qualifications you require create disadvantages for candidates who aren't from academic backgrounds. Work to eliminate bias that would rule out viable finalists based on arbitrary and often coded standards such as "cultural fit." Give extra consideration to internal candidates and their growth potential. Understand the unique challenges they face in applying for the position at the school. If they are not selected at your school, encourage them to apply elsewhere.

When working with aspiring leaders who are in roles that aren't in the traditional pipeline to headship, offer them opportunities to be involved in fundraising, financial planning, the budgeting process, and strategic decision-making to help them develop headship skills. Be intentional in providing mentors and career sponsors for aspiring leaders.

When negotiating head salaries and benefits, use DASL and other NAIS tools to benchmark the salaries and benefits you offer with schools like yours and heads with similar experience. Be aware of the existence of implicit bias when setting salaries. For example, when women request a higher salary, they may be perceived as pushy or difficult, while men may be seen as having good negotiation skills.

To ensure a comprehensive approach to diversity, equity, inclusion, and racial and social justice in your school community, start from the inside out. Ground the work in your school's mission and core values so members of the community can see themselves and others in your efforts. Create a structure of support and accountability to advance the work, hire dedicated staff, and provide an ample budget for the office/department. Remember the maxim, "We measure what we value." Make DEI work as fundamental to your school as admissions, student affairs, advancement, etc. Lead the work with equal commitment.

Work with your trustees to develop a board-level DEI committee. Support the board in developing and implementing research-based board inclusion behaviors and other policies and practices that support and enhance the school's strategic goals and objectives.

Conduct periodic climate assessments, equity audits, and student and faculty/staff health and well-being surveys. See Resources for more information about the tools NAIS offers.

Initiate or continue to host regular DEI professional development for all faculty and staff. Integrate these sessions into your overall professional development so educators can make cross-disciplinary and other connections.

 ## Resources

"Diversity and Inclusion," Deloitte:
https://www2.deloitte.com/us/en/insights/topics/value-of-diversity-and-inclusion.html

"Diversity and Inclusion," McKinsey & Company:
https://www.mckinsey.com/featured-insights/diversity-and-inclusion

NAIS Assessment of Inclusivity and Multiculturalism (AIM):
https://www.nais.org/analyze/assessment-of-inclusivity-and-multiculturalism/

NAIS Data and Analysis for School Leadership (DASL):
https://dasl.nais.org/

NAIS Snapshot Surveys:
https://www.nais.org/articles/pages/member/research/nais-snapshot-survey/

***People of Color and White Women in Independent School Headship*, NAIS:**
https://www.nais.org/media/MemberDocuments/Research/NAIS_Research_HeadshipReport2018.pdf

***Women in the Workplace 2020*, Sarah Coury et al., McKinsey & Company:**
https://www.mckinsey.com/featured-insights/diversity-and-inclusion/women-in-the-workplace

ENDNOTES

[1] Bill Hussar et al., *The Condition of Education 2020* (Washington, DC: National Center for Education Statistics, U.S. Department of Education, 2020); online at https://nces.ed.gov/pubs2020/2020144.pdf. Jason A. Grissom et al., "Unequal Pay for Equal Work? Unpacking

the Gender Gap in Principal Compensation," *Economics of Education Review*, June 2021; online at https://www.sciencedirect.com/science/article/abs/pii/S0272775721000339.

[2] NAIS, "#Black@ Movement," NAIS Snapshot, Week of September 21, 2020; online at https://www.nais.org/getmedia/df973c51-a294-4a1c-82f5-e443d76bd48c/NAISsnapshotSurvey092520.pdf.

[3] Anuli Ononye and Jackson Walker, "The States Taking Steps to Ban Critical Race Theory," *The Hill*, June 9, 2021; online at https://thehill.com/homenews/state-watch/557571-the-states-taking-steps-to-ban-critical-race-theory.

[4] Hussar et al., *The Condition of Education*.

[5] Sarah Coury et al., *Women in the Workplace 2020* (McKinsey & Company, 2020); online at https://www.mckinsey.com/featured-insights/diversity-and-inclusion/women-in-the-workplace.

[6] Hussar et al., *The Condition of Education*.

[7] NAIS, *People of Color and White Women in Independent School Headship* (Washington, DC: 2018); online at https://www.nais.org/media/MemberDocuments/Research/NAIS_Research_HeadshipReport2018.pdf.

[8] Grissom et al., "Unequal Pay for Equal Work?"

[9] Larry Buchanan, Quoctrung Bui, and Jugal K. Patel, "Black Lives Matter May Be the Largest Movement in U.S. History," *The New York Times*, July 3, 2020; online at https://www.nytimes.com/interactive/2020/07/03/us/george-floyd-protests-crowd-size.html.

[10] David Isaacs et al., "Editorial: Black Lives Matter Movement: The Time for Nice Words and Good Intentions Is Over," *Journal of Paediatrics and Child Health*, 56 (2020); online at https://onlinelibrary.wiley.com/doi/epdf/10.1111/jpc.15100.

[11] NAIS, "#Black@ Movement," September 2020.

[12] Ibid.

[13] Stephen Sawchuk, "What Is Critical Race Theory, and Why Is It Under Attack?" *Education Week*, May 18, 2021; online at https://www.edweek.org/leadership/what-is-critical-race-theory-and-why-is-it-under-attack/2021/05.

[14] Ononye and Walker, "The States Taking Steps."

[15] Janel George, "A Lesson on Critical Race Theory," American Bar Association, January 12, 2021; online at https://www.americanbar.org/groups/crsj/publications/human_rights_magazine_home/civil-rights-reimagining-policing/a-lesson-on-critical-race-theory/.

[16] *Education Week*, "Map: Where Critical Race Theory Is Under Attack," July 15, 2021; online at https://www.edweek.org/policy-politics/map-where-critical-race-theory-is-under-attack/2021/06.

[17] Alice Korngold, "Insights for Action: Diversity, Equity, and Inclusion (DEI): Lessons for Business from Nonprofit Boards," *Better World Leadership Reports*, 2020; online at https://alicekorngold.com/wp-content/uploads/2020/12/2020-Better-World-Leadership-Report.pdf?_hsfp=2237438867&_hssc=251652889.1.1625782796773&_hstc=251652889.554591a98b5a3119c50e31c1446e0592.1625782796772.1625782796772.1625782796772.1.

[18] NAIS, "Leadership, Governance, and DEI," NAIS Snapshot, Week of March 29, 2021; online at https://www.nais.org/getmedia/060d7364-49d2-4b64-b61e-ff013fcdce30/NAISsnapshotSurvey040221DEI.pdf.

The
WELL-BEING
Outlook

By Carol Bernate and Myra McGovern

**Carol Bernate is
a research associate
at NAIS.**

**Myra McGovern is
vice president of media.**

TRENDING
FOR 2021-2022

- Independent school students are highly engaged, but stress, anxiety, and depression threaten to undermine achievement.

- Students rely heavily on teachers for emotional support; teachers need assistance to provide it.

- Despite concerns about pandemic-related learning loss, experts urge schools to avoid emphasizing academic rigor at the expense of students' well-being.

Even in the midst of the disruption caused by the COVID-19 pandemic, research has identified a bright spot for independent school students: They continue to show high levels of academic engagement, characterized by active involvement in learning and in their community and associated with the skills they need to thrive in college and beyond.

Even so, teachers report that they've observed students suffering from a number of pandemic-related concerns, ranging from academic stress and anxiety to worries about family health. These concerns coincide with research that shows a downward trend in students' resilience-related skills.

To help with these problems, many schools have called upon teachers to support students' health and well-being in new ways. This added responsibility has taken a toll on educators, who report that their own mental health has suffered.

Concerns about learning loss have also dominated headlines, with many blaming online learning, poor internet access, and student trauma for the achievement deficits.[1] As many schools and districts consider ways to accelerate instruction to help students catch up, experts also stress the importance of supporting students' well-being to help them learn and thrive.

Students Are Highly Engaged and Continue to Achieve, But Resilience-Related Skills Are Lagging

Students in NAIS schools continue to report high levels of engagement. They take pride in their schoolwork and put forth considerable effort to achieve.[2]

But teachers note the toll that striving for high academic achievement can take on their students; 98% of NAIS teachers polled in a survey of student and teacher wellness reported academic stress or anxiety among students during the pandemic. Other disruptions, like fear related to caregiver absence and physical safety and security, were also common among students at NAIS schools (Figure 1).[3] In addition, the effects of recent economic, social, and political instability are likely to complicate student learning for the foreseeable future.[4]

FIGURE 1: **Student Concerns During the Pandemic, Reported by Teachers**

PERCENTAGE OF TEACHERS NOTICING CHALLENGES AMONG STUDENTS IN NAIS SCHOOLS

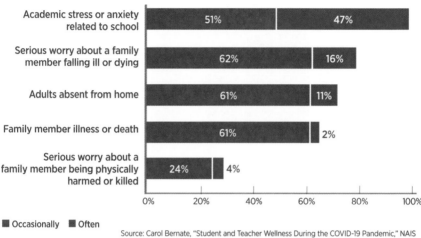

■ Occasionally   ■ Often

Source: Carol Bernate, "Student and Teacher Wellness During the COVID-19 Pandemic," NAIS

According to a 2020 survey of student resilience by Authentic Connections, 5.5% of NAIS students in grades six through 12 showed clinically significant levels of depression, and 5.6% showed symptoms of anxiety. But rates varied for students from different racial and ethnic backgrounds. While African American students in the study reported lower rates of clinical anxiety than their peers and comparable rates of depression (Figure 2), wellness is measured over several variables, and the study found that Latinx and multiracial students are the most at risk for learning obstacles related to mental health. These findings are in line with other studies that showed that stress and anxiety were greater obstacles to learning for Black, Hispanic, and multiracial students than for white and Asian students, and data collected nationally by YouthTruth identifies feelings of anxiety and stress as the Number 1 obstacle to learning for all students in 2021.[5]

The consulting firm McKinsey & Company identifies resilience as central to community recovery from upheavals, such as the 2008 financial crisis and the COVID-19 pandemic.[6] Industry leaders recognize deep understanding of the self as an important tool to develop resilience, according to *Harvard Business Review*.[7] However, student engagement data indicate a downward trend in the development of resilience-related skills at NAIS schools in recent years. Seventy-two percent of the participants in the 2020 High School Survey of Student

FIGURE 2: Rates of Depression and Anxiety* Among Students at NAIS Schools, by Race and Ethnicity, 2020

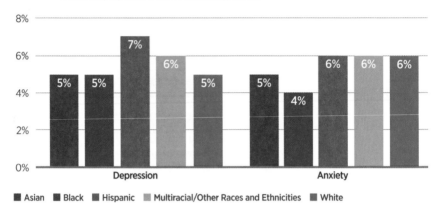

* Clinically significant symptoms

Source: Authentic Connections, "Student and Faculty Resilience During COVID: Fostering Well-Being Using Data Driven Interventions"

Engagement said that their school helped them develop their personal beliefs and values, and 67% said that their school contributed to their understanding of themselves (Figure 3). These numbers are down from 2016 levels of 78% and 71%, respectively. Levels of effort in schoolwork remain high (86%), but fewer students connect their current work to future success (61% compared to 64% in 2016) (Figure 4).[8]

FIGURE 3: School's Role in Students' Personal Growth, 2016 and 2020

STUDENTS WHO ATTRIBUTED DEVELOPMENT OF SKILLS TO THEIR SCHOOL "SOME" OR "VERY MUCH"

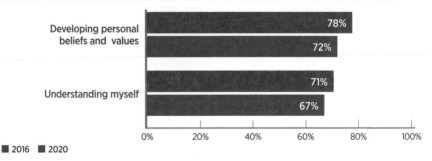

Sources: Joseph Corbett and Amada Torres, "NAIS Report on the 2016 High School Survey of Student Engagement" and Margaret Anne Rowe, "NAIS Report on the 2020 High School Survey of Student Engagement"

FIGURE 4: **Student Effort, 2016 and 2020**

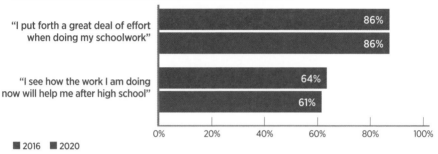

STUDENTS AGREEING OR STRONGLY AGREEING WITH THE STATEMENTS

"I put forth a great deal of effort when doing my schoolwork" — 86% / 86%

"I see how the work I am doing now will help me after high school" — 64% / 61%

■ 2016 ■ 2020

Sources: Joseph Corbett and Amada Torres, "NAIS Report on the 2016 High School Survey of Student Engagement" and Margaret Anne Rowe, "NAIS Report on the 2020 High School Survey of Student Engagement"

Teachers Provide Crucial Support to Students, But Heavy Demands Have Implications for Burnout and Teacher Retention

Students rely on the emotional support of their teachers to achieve. Participants in the 2020 survey of student resilience identified emotional support from school faculty as one of the most important elements of their recent school experience. Despite taking satisfaction in their ability to help their students, most teachers who participated in the survey also reported feeling overwhelmed. Ninety-five percent of teachers reported that when a mental health challenge arises for their students, teachers often take initiative to provide emotional support, and 93% reported feeling overwhelmed by seemingly endless responsibility (Figure 5).[9]

FIGURE 5: **Views of NAIS Teachers During the Pandemic**

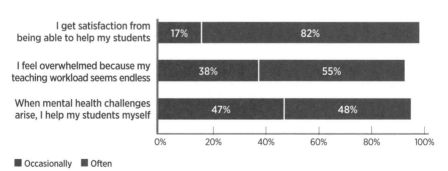

I get satisfaction from being able to help my students — 17% / 82%

I feel overwhelmed because my teaching workload seems endless — 38% / 55%

When mental health challenges arise, I help my students myself — 47% / 48%

■ Occasionally ■ Often

Source: Carol Bernate, "Student and Teacher Wellness During the COVID-19 Pandemic," NAIS

FIGURE 6: **Teachers' Sense of Preparedness During the Pandemic**

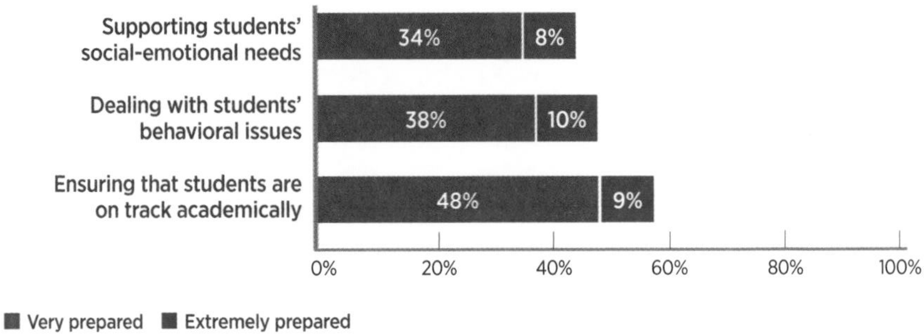

Category	Very prepared	Extremely prepared
Supporting students' social-emotional needs	34%	8%
Dealing with students' behavioral issues	38%	10%
Ensuring that students are on track academically	48%	9%

■ Very prepared ■ Extremely prepared

Source: Carol Bernate, "NAIS COVID-19 Staff Reopening Survey: Perceptions of Reopening Across School Groups," NAIS

Further, of the functions required in the role, teachers feel *least* equipped to provide the emotional support upon which students rely. In the 2020 NAIS Staff Reopening Survey, just 8% of teachers felt extremely well prepared to support students' emotional needs when they returned to school after COVID-19 closures. And just 10% or fewer felt extremely well prepared to deal with student behavioral issues or with ensuring that students stayed on track academically (Figure 6).[10]

Research has shown the importance of teacher well-being. Healthy educators are more available, engaged, and confident in their roles. They have the emotional availability to support positive student outcomes.[11] In addition, they are more likely to strive to improve their performance and less likely to need time off or to seek new roles.[12] In contrast, the emotional demands the pandemic has placed on teachers are associated with burnout, and teachers report that they need help.[13] Schools are in the best position to retain their teachers when teachers feel that they have help managing both their workload and their students' well-being.[14]

Experts Recommend Focusing on Student Well-Being to Mitigate Learning Loss

In March 2021, McKinsey & Company reported that "learning loss is global— and significant."[15] An earlier McKinsey report (from December 2020) projected that "students on average could lose five to nine months of learning by the end of June 2021." Older students were more likely than younger students to experience greater learning loss—measured by students' standardized test scores in 2020-2021 compared to historic averages. Because of systemic inequities, the national average scores for students of color showed greater loss than those of white students.[16]

In *Learning During COVID-19: Initial Findings on Students' Reading and Math Achievement and Growth*, released in November 2020, the Northwest Evaluation Association found that students performed similarly in reading achievement, but the average test scores in math dropped 5 to 10 percentage points between 2019 and 2020.[17]

Independent school families may feel differently about learning loss depending on their motivations for enrolling their children in independent schools. A national, quantitative analysis done by NAIS found that only 19% of parents were looking for a school that could challenge their talented children and help them get into a college that was elite academically (Ivy League) or athletically (Division I). A larger segment of the parent body (31%) sought schools that would challenge and engage their children but that were not so rigorous that they would cause unhealthy stress. The remaining segments of the parent body valued a balanced approach over academic rigor for the sake of a resume.[18]

While some families may choose independent schools for academic rigor, aggressively pursuing academic goals during and immediately after the pandemic can also have negative consequences for mental health.

"Though millions of students may have fallen behind academically, administrators need to refrain from prioritizing academic achievement above all else," writes Scott Poland, a professor at the College of Psychology and director of the Suicide and Violence Prevention Office at Nova Southeastern University in Florida. "Students will need time to process their trauma and experiences of the last year. With more than 500,000 deaths from COVID-19, it's inevitable students will still be grieving for lost family, friends and neighbors."[19] Further, heightening academic pressure as students are trying to cope with challenges brought on by the pandemic could exacerbate students' existing mental health issues.[20]

Although some may worry that social and emotional learning takes time away from accelerated academics or catch-up work, experts suggest that focusing on student well-being is a key strategy to mitigate learning loss. Like strengthening community and building interpersonal connections, social-emotional learning builds important foundations for learning.[21] Laying these foundations presents an opportunity for independent schools that make educating the whole child a key component of their missions.

Strategic Questions

How do you measure student engagement at your school?

How has the pandemic affected your students' mental health? How does the impact vary by grade and among students from different demographic groups?

In what ways could you better support student health and well-being? How would you measure the impact of your initiatives?

How do you evaluate the needs and satisfaction of teachers?

How does your school gauge learning from year to year? What differences did the pandemic year show?

How do you communicate with families who are concerned about learning loss?

How might you reimagine your school to place a focus on student and adult well-being at the center? As a report by Deloitte notes: "Organizations that integrate well-being into the design of work at the individual, team, and organizational levels will build a sustainable future where workers can feel and perform at their best."[22]

Action Steps

Consider tools to evaluate student health and well-being, such as the Independent School Health Check survey (available late fall 2021).

Survey teachers about their emotional health, and evaluate what types of supports the school could offer.

Determine how equipped teachers feel to support students' social and emotional needs. If student needs are outstripping teachers' capacity, consider designating a staff member to coordinate extra student support.

Using NAIS's Jobs-to-Be-Done research on independent school parents, evaluate why families select your school. Review NAIS's "Learning Loss and Independent School Students: A Jobs-to-Be-Done Perspective" to better address families' needs and wants.

Resources

Independent School Health Check:
https://www.nais.org/analyze/independent-school-health-check/

"Jobs-to-Be-Done Study on Independent School Parents," NAIS:
https://www.nais.org/articles/pages/research/nais-research-jobs-to-be-done-study-on-independent-school-parents/

"Jobs-to-Be-Done Study on Independent School Teachers," NAIS:
https://www.nais.org/articles/pages/research/nais-research-jobs-to-be-done-study-on-independent-school-teachers/

"Learning Loss and Independent School Students: A Jobs-to-Be-Done Perspective," NAIS:
https://www.nais.org/articles/pages/member/research/nais-research-learning-loss-and-independent-school-students-a-jobs-to-be-done-perspective/

"Retaining and Attracting Teachers Amid COVID-19: A Jobs-to-Be-Done Perspective," NAIS:
https://www.nais.org/articles/pages/member/research/retaining-and-attracting-teachers-amid-covid-19-a-jobs-to-be-done-perspective/

Student Engagement Surveys, NAIS:
https://www.nais.org/analyze/student-engagement-surveys/

ENDNOTES

[1] Tom Armelino, "As Schools Go to Distance Learning, Key Strategies to Prevent Learning Loss," EdSource, July 17, 2020; online at https://edsource.org/2020/as-schools-go-to-distance-learning-key-strategies-to-prevent-learning-loss/636196. Brian Soika, "How Should Schools Address Learning Loss?" USC Rossier School of Education, April 1, 2021; online at https://rossier.usc.edu/how-should-schools-address-learning-loss/.

[2] Margaret Anne Rowe, "NAIS Report on the 2020 High School Survey of Student Engagement," NAIS, October 2020; online at https://www.nais.org/articles/pages/research/nais-report-on-the-2020-high-school-survey-of-student-engagement/.

[3] Carol Bernate, "Student and Teacher Wellness During the COVID-19 Pandemic," NAIS, November 2020; online at https://www.nais.org/articles/pages/research/nais-research-student-and-teacher-wellness-during-the-covid-19-pandemic/.

[4] Arianna Prothero, "The Pandemic Will Affect Students' Mental Health for Years to Come. How Schools Can Help," *Education Week*, March 31, 2021; online at https://www.edweek.org/leadership/the-pandemic-will-affect-students-mental-health-for-years-to-come-how-schools-can-help/2021/03.

[5] Authentic Connections, "Student and Faculty Resilience During COVID: Fostering Well-

Being Using Data Driven Intervention," forthcoming. YouthTruth, *Students Weigh In, Part II: Learning & Well-Being During COVID-19* (San Francisco and Cambridge, MA: 2021); online at https://youthtruthsurvey.org/students-weigh-in-part2/.

[6] Erica Hutchins Coe and Kana Enomoto, "Returning to Resilience: The Impact of COVID-19 on Mental Health and Substance Use," McKinsey & Company, April 2, 2021; online at https://www.mckinsey.com/industries/healthcare-systems-and-services/our-insights/returning-to-resilience-the-impact-of-covid-19-on-behavioral-health.

[7] Ron Carucci, "The Better You Know Yourself, the More Resilient You'll Be," *Harvard Business Review*, September 2017; online at https://hbr.org/2017/09/the-better-you-know-yourself-the-more-resilient-youll-be.

[8] Joseph Corbett and Amada Torres, "NAIS Report on the 2016 High School Survey of Student Engagement," NAIS, July 2017; online at https://www.nais.org/articles/pages/research/2016-nais-report-on-the-high-school-survey-of-student-engagement/. Rowe, "NAIS Report on the 2020 High School Survey of Student Engagement."

[9] Authentic Connections, "Student and Faculty Resilience During COVID."

[10] Carol Bernate, "NAIS COVID-19 Staff Reopening Survey: Perceptions of Reopening Across School Groups," NAIS, 2021; online at https://www.nais.org/articles/pages/research/nais-covid-19-staff-reopening-survey-perceptions-of-reopening-across-school-groups/.

[11] Gallup, "How to Improve Student and Educator Wellbeing," 2021; online at Gallup.com/education.

[12] Arnold B. Bakker and Wilmar B. Schaufeli, "Burnout Contagion Processes Among Teachers," *Journal of Applied Social Psychology*, November 2000; online at https://www.researchgate.net/publication/227799025_Burnout_Contagion_Processes_Among_Teachers1. Gallup, "How to Improve Student and Educator Wellbeing."

[13] Authentic Connections, "Student and Faculty Resilience During COVID."

[14] NAIS, "Jobs-to-Be-Done Study on Independent School Teachers"; online at https://www.nais.org/articles/pages/research/nais-research-jobs-to-be-done-study-on-independent-school-teachers/.

[15] Li-Kai Chen et al., "Teacher Survey: Learning Loss Is Global—and Significant," McKinsey & Company, March 1, 2021; online at https://www.mckinsey.com/industries/public-and-social-sector/our-insights/teacher-survey-learning-loss-is-global-and-significant.

[16] Emma Dorn et al., "COVID-19 and Learning Loss—Disparities Grow and Students Need Help," McKinsey & Company, December 8, 2020; online at https://www.mckinsey.com/industries/public-and-social-sector/our-insights/covid-19-and-learning-loss-disparities-grow-and-students-need-help.

[17] Megan Kuhfeld et al., *Learning During COVID-19: Initial Findings on Students' Reading and Math Achievement and Growth* (Portland, OR: Northwest Evaluation Association, 2020); online at https://www.nwea.org/research/center/collaborative-for-student-growth/.

[18] NAIS, "Why Parents Choose Independent Schools: A Quantitative Analysis"; online at https://www.nais.org/getmedia/b0a28162-e0b4-4451-ad2f-15943485d5fc/NAIS-Research_-Parent-JTBD_QuantSummary_8-28-20.pdf.

[19] Scott Poland, "As Schools Reopen, Prioritizing Student Mental Health Can Prevent 'Twin-Demic,'" *K-12 Dive*, March 25, 2021; online at https://www.k12dive.com/news/as-schools-reopen-prioritizing-student-mental-health-can-prevent-twin-dem/597332/?utm_source=Sailthru&utm_medium=email&utm_campaign=Issue:%202021-03-25%20K-12%20Dive%20%5Bissue:33227%5D&utm_term=K-12%20Dive.

[20] Kelly Glass, "Kids Need Less Academic Pressure and More Support After a Year of Isolation and Learning Losses," *The Washington Post*, April 23, 2021; online at https://www.washingtonpost.com/lifestyle/2021/04/23/learning-losses-academic-pressure-mental-health/?utm_campaign=wp_on_parenting&utm_medium=email&utm_source=newsletter&wpisrc=nl_parent&carta-url=https%3A%2F%2Fs2.washingtonpost.com%2Fcar-ln-tr%2F32019f2%2F6082ef389d2fda39cec6b4bb%2F5e4ec80eae7e8a0d542d276a%2F21%2F75%2F6082ef389d2fda39cec6b4bb.

[21] Armelino, "As Schools Go to Distance Learning." Julie Mason, "What Schools Can Do to Make Up for COVID-19 Learning Loss," We Are Teachers, September 14, 2020; online at https://www.weareteachers.com/make-up-for-covid-19-learning-loss/. Soika, "How Should Schools Address Learning Loss?"

[22] Erica Volini et al., "Diving Deeper: Five Workforce Trends to Watch in 2021," Deloitte, December 9, 2020; online at https://www2.deloitte.com/us/en/insights/focus/human-capital-trends/2021/workforce-trends-2020.html.

The
LEARNING AND
TEACHING
Outlook

By Tim Fish and Jackie Wolking

**Tim Fish is
chief innovation officer
at NAIS.**

**Jackie Wolking is
director of innovation
programs.**

TRENDING
FOR 2021-2022

- Some schools and districts are likely to continue offering online learning options for students after the pandemic.

- The focus on social-emotional learning grew during the pandemic.

- Some schools may continue aspects of virtual professional development for teachers.

I n the 2020-2021 school year, educators were forced to reimagine almost every aspect of the school experience to meet the unique challenges posed by the pandemic. The way schools delivered education fluctuated over time, with many offering distance learning or a hybrid model at some point (Figure 1). But by early May 2021, 83% of independent schools were operating fully in person,[1] compared to 54% of public schools.[2]

As schools look ahead, they face these questions: What aspects of the pandemic year will remain? What will be abandoned? And what new methods of teaching and learning will emerge?

Early indicators signal that the return to the classroom doesn't mean an end to all of the changes the pandemic brought about. Virtual learning is likely to continue under some circumstances because it has practical uses, meets market demand, and allows schools to make use of the tools and training they've invested in. The increased focus on social-emotional programming that took place during the pandemic may also continue to be valuable and even enhance academic achievement.

In addition, schools may find online professional development to be an economical way to hone teachers' skills while taking advantage of their increased ability to work with technology. And slowly emerging changes in hiring priorities hint at a demand for greater proficiency in teaching in a virtual setting as well as more flexible working conditions.

Online Learning Options for Students Are Likely to Remain Post-Pandemic

Even though almost all independent schools had returned to in-person learning by May 2021, many foresaw circumstances in which they would maintain online learning options in the future. Fifty-four percent of school leaders polled in an NAIS Snapshot Survey said that online/distance learning would continue to be an alternative offering for the 2021-2022 school year. They considered granting

FIGURE 1: **Changes to Learning Model Over School Year 2020-2021**

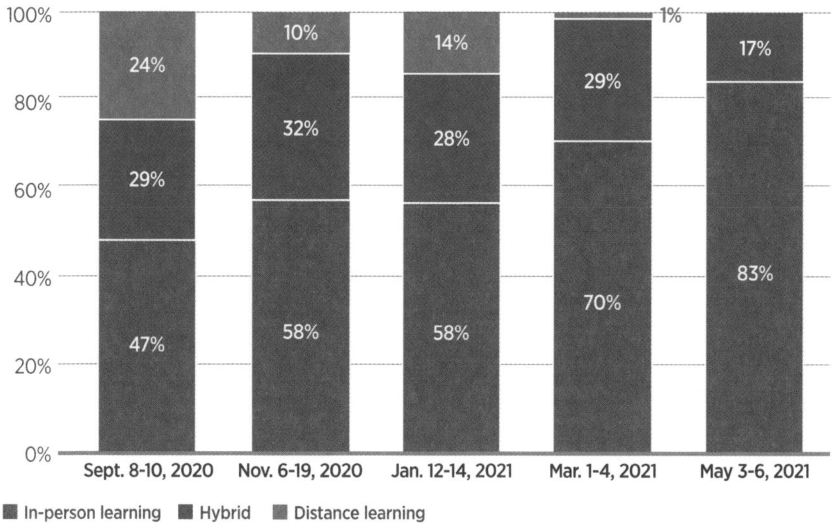

	Sept. 8-10, 2020	Nov. 6-19, 2020	Jan. 12-14, 2021	Mar. 1-4, 2021	May 3-6, 2021
Distance learning	24%	10%	14%	1%	17%
Hybrid	29%	32%	28%	29%	
In-person learning	47%	58%	58%	70%	83%

■ In-person learning ■ Hybrid ■ Distance learning

Results represent unique groupings of schools, not the same schools surveyed over time.

Source: NAIS Snapshot, "Planning for 2021-2022 and Beyond," May 2021

synchronous, remote access to classes for a variety of reasons, including illness, family emergencies, and snow days (Figure 2).[3]

Independent schools aren't the only ones that are likely to retain virtual learning in some circumstances. A Rand Corporation report titled *Remote Learn-*

FIGURE 2: **Reasons Schools Would Grant Remote Access to Classes in 2021-2022**

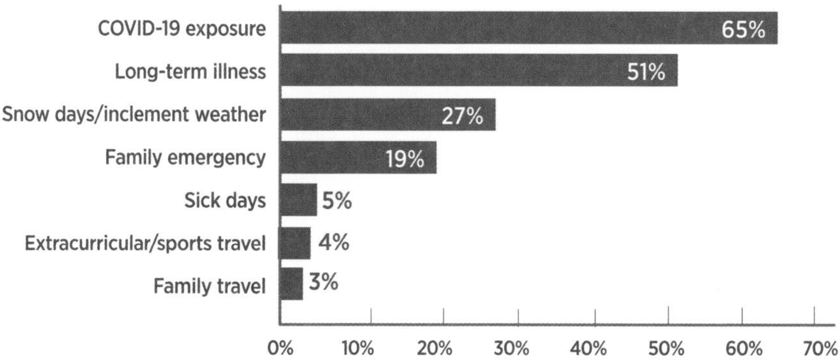

COVID-19 exposure	65%
Long-term illness	51%
Snow days/inclement weather	27%
Family emergency	19%
Sick days	5%
Extracurricular/sports travel	4%
Family travel	3%

Source: NAIS Snapshot, "Planning for 2021-2022 and Beyond," May 2021

ing Is Here to Stay found that "about two in ten [public school] districts have already adopted, plan to adopt, or are considering adopting virtual schools as part of their district portfolio after the end of the COVID-19 pandemic." These districts cited student and parent demand as one factor driving their decision.[4]

Higher education has also seen continued demand for remote access. In an April 2021 Digital Learning Pulse survey, 73% of college students polled said they "somewhat" or "strongly" agreed that they would like to take an online course in the future.[5]

Another factor may drive continued interest in virtual learning. Many independent schools made considerable investments in technology during the pandemic. A June 2020 NAIS Snapshot Survey found that 39% of independent schools upgraded or purchased new devices for faculty and staff, 33% upgraded their digital infrastructure, and 85% provided additional teacher training on online learning design and best practices.[6] Given the money and time they've devoted to virtual learning, many schools are probably wondering whether the investment was simply an unavoidable cost of the pandemic or whether these tech-focused assets can be leveraged in useful ways in the years to come.

Schools Are Increasing Their Focus on Social-Emotional Learning

Along with shifting learning models, many students experienced heightened levels of uncertainty, stress, and anxiety. Sixty percent of independent school leaders said that student mental health worsened during the pandemic (see Chapter 9, "The Well-Being Outlook"). As a result, many schools modified their offerings to focus on well-being. The modifications included increased check-ins with advisers and teachers, expanded social-emotional curricula, and more counseling services (Figure 3).[7]

These increases in social-emotional programming came in response to the pandemic. But, like virtual learning, expanded well-being programs may prove useful in the future. Integrating this approach more broadly and permanently has been shown to improve students' academic success.[8] A 2017 Aspen Institute brief, *The Evidence Base for How We Learn: Supporting Students' Social, Emotional, and Academic Development*, reported that school-based programming that was focused on social and emotional development made a positive difference in children's academic achievement and behavior.[9]

FIGURE 3: School Programming to Support Student Well-Being, 2020

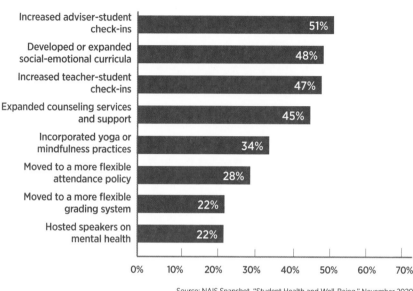

Source: NAIS Snapshot, "Student Health and Well-Being," November 2020

Teachers Are Developing New Skills Through New Means

Students were not the only ones to experience major changes during the pandemic. In addition to reframing what and how they taught, teachers changed the ways they met with other educators and honed their own skills. Some educators plan to continue using these new methods. As of May 2021, 27% of independent school leaders said that they would run school-led professional development virtually in the 2021-2022 school year, even though the school would be in person. Seventeen percent said they would run faculty/staff meetings virtually.[10]

The numbers were far bigger for public schools. The EdWeek Research Center reported that 41% of public school teachers, principals, and district leaders who had eliminated in-person professional development events during the pandemic thought this trend was likely to continue.[11]

There are two reasons for schools to continue to use online meetings in the future.

Virtual professional development is economical.[12] With 73% of independent schools reporting that they had decreased or frozen professional development budgets for 2020-2021,[13] hosting outside experts or even school-led retreats virtually could provide an attractive alternative that dramatically reduces costs, such as venue fees, travel, and lodging.

Teachers have become more proficient with online tools. With a majority of schools using tools like Zoom or Google Meets to conduct virtual interactions,[14] most teachers have the technological skills needed to successfully navigate this form of adult learning. In a survey by the EdWeek Research Center, 77% of the respondents reported that their use of video conferencing grew "a lot stronger" during the pandemic.[15]

According to a January 2021 NAIS Snapshot Survey, the changes in teaching and learning may also bring about shifts in hiring and in the nature of work for teachers. Two-thirds of the independent school leaders who responded to the survey said that, when hiring, they were prioritizing candidates who were able to adapt to new ways of teaching. More than half of the survey respondents prioritized candidates proficient in classroom technologies, and almost a quarter prioritized those with online teaching experience (Figure 4).[16]

Other responses pointed to changes that are happening to a lesser degree but are still noteworthy. Twenty-one percent of independent school leaders said they were offering more interim positions, and 6% were offering remote job options.[17] For educators, these small shifts could evolve into a more flexible employment landscape—one that's rich with part-time, virtual, and hybrid opportunities for teachers as well as for students.

FIGURE 4: Skills Prioritized by Schools in Hiring for 2021-2022

Which of the following, if any, are you prioritizing in your evaluation process of teacher candidates to a greater extent than before the pandemic? (Percentage of respondents answering yes)

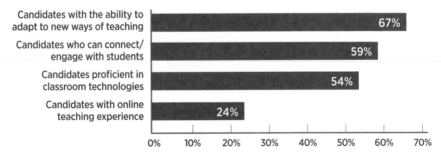

Source: NAIS Snapshot, "Teacher Hiring and Attrition Rates," January 2021

Strategic Questions

How might you leverage online learning resources and partnerships to increase learning opportunities for current students or to attract new students to the school?

In what ways could you better connect with part-time teachers or staff? What opportunities exist to offer remote work options for non-teaching staff?

What would school look like if well-being were at the center? Are there opportunities to rethink the school schedule? How might you offer more flexibility to students (e.g., some asynchronous learning days or late-start days)? How might your approach differ by age group?

What will the ideal classroom design look like if some aspects of hybrid learning remain? How can you best leverage the power of technology to better connect the classroom to outside learners and resources?

How should you use remote tools like Zoom in the future?

Action Steps

Survey or interview parents, teachers, and students to discover what aspects of pandemic learning were most effective and to present potential innovation opportunities for the future.

Connect with peer schools to learn about new learning models.

Consult the NAIS Jobs-to-Be-Done research on parents and teachers to discover the "Jobs" that are most prevalent in your school and to help ensure that your innovations align with parent and teacher expectations.

Consider participating in the NAIS Strategy Lab to learn about tools and frameworks that support your post-pandemic innovation designs.

In designing online professional development for teachers, focus on skills that are easily transferrable in a classroom setting and on content that is "practical, concrete, and readily usable, rather than theoretical."[18]

Brainstorm opportunities for partnerships with other schools and organizations to enhance learning opportunities and improve efficiency.

Resources

"Educating Children Remotely: A Focus on Social-Emotional Learning," Hannah Ellerbeck, NYU Institute of Human Development and Social Change:
https://steinhardt.nyu.edu/ihdsc/on-the-ground/educating-children-remotely

"How Schools Can Redeploy Teachers in Creative Ways During COVID-19," Catherine Gewertz, *Education Week*:
https://www.edweek.org/leadership/how-schools-can-redeploy-teachers-in-creative-ways-during-covid-19/2020/08

NAIS Strategy Lab:
https://strategylab.nais.org

Optimizing EdTech for an Expanded Definition of Student Success, Molly B. Zielezinski et al., MBZ Labs:
https://secureservercdn.net/166.62.110.60/mb9.11f.myftpupload.com/wp-content/uploads/2020/02/Optimizing-EdTech-for-Student-Success_MBZLabs2020.pdf?time=1597219334

"Supports for Social and Emotional Learning in Schools," Laura S. Hamilton and Christopher Joseph Doss, RAND Corporation:
https://www.rand.org/pubs/research_briefs/RBA397-1.html

ENDNOTES

[1] NAIS, "Planning for 2021-2022 and Beyond," NAIS Snapshot, Week of May 3, 2021; online at https://www.nais.org/getmedia/2b954bb9-e4ee-4958-b69c-0429b1749f48/NAISsnapshotsurvey050721.pdf.

[2] Institute of Education Sciences, "Monthly School Survey Dashboard," March 2021, U.S. Department of Education; online at https://ies.ed.gov/schoolsurvey/. The survey included elementary and middle schools.

[3] NAIS, "Planning for 2021-2022," May 2021.

[4] Heather L. Schwartz et al., *Remote Learning Is Here to Stay: Results from the First American School District Panel Survey* (Santa Monica, CA: Rand Corporation, 2020), p. 1; online at https://www.rand.org/pubs/research_reports/RRA956-1.html.

[5] Lindsay McKenzie, "Students Want Online Learning Options Post-Pandemic," *Inside Higher Ed*, April 27, 2021; online at https://www.insidehighered.com/news/2021/04/27/survey-reveals-positive-outlook-online-instruction-post-pandemic.

[6] NAIS, "Online Learning," NAIS Snapshot, Week of June 29, 2020; online at https://www.nais.org/getmedia/b46dd943-3845-4ea4-882a-4b4fac1a7576/NAIS-Snapshot-Survey_Online-Learning_7-2-20.pdf.

[7] NAIS, "Student Health and Well-Being," NAIS Snapshot, Week of November 16, 2020; online at https://www.nais.org/getmedia/1e267524-90b6-4edd-959b-6bb7666b22b3/

NAISsnapshotStudentHealth112020.pdf.

[8] Joseph A. Durlak et al., "The Impact of Enhancing Students' Social and Emotional Learning: A Meta-Analysis of School-Based Universal Interventions," *Child Development*, January/February 2011, pp. 405-432; online at https://casel.org/wp-content/uploads/2016/01/meta-analysis-child-development-1.pdf.

[9] Stephanie M. Jones and Jennifer Kahn, *The Evidence Base for How We Learn: Supporting Students' Social, Emotional, and Academic Development* (Washington, DC: Aspen Institute, National Commission on Social, Emotional, and Academic Development, 2017); online at https://www.aspeninstitute.org/publications/evidence-base-learn/.

[10] NAIS, "Planning for 2021-2022," May 2021.

[11] Kevin Bushweller and Sterling C. Lloyd, "How the Pandemic Is Shaping K-12 Education (in Charts)," *Education Week*, April 1, 2021; online at https://www.edweek.org/leadership/how-the-pandemic-is-shaping-k-12-education-in-charts/2021/04.

[12] Ibid.

[13] NAIS, "Staffing and Finances," NAIS Snapshot, Week of November 16, 2020; online at https://www.nais.org/getmedia/d372b0a1-aebe-4acf-8800-cd80ae15a3e1/NAIS_Snapshot-Survey_Staffing-Finances_11-20-20.pdf.

[14] NAIS, "Online Learning," June 2020.

[15] Alyson Klein, "'A Year of Tremendous Growth.' How the Pandemic Forced Teachers to Master Technology," *Education Week*, April 20, 2021; online at https://www.edweek.org/technology/a-year-of-tremendous-growth-how-the-pandemic-forced-teachers-to-master-technology/2021/04.

[16] NAIS, "Teacher Hiring and Attrition Rates," NAIS Snapshot, Week of January 11, 2021; online at http://www.nais.org/getmedia/927663e5-e878-4a6c-85a4-fd980beaa412/naissnapshot011521hiring.pdf.

[17] Ibid.

[18] Todd D. Reeves and Joseph J. Pedulla, "Bolstering the Impact of Online Professional Development for Teachers," *The Journal of Educational Research & Policy Studies*, February 2013, p. 62; online at https://files.eric.ed.gov/fulltext/ED545314.pdf.

EPILOGUE

By Donna Orem

If there's one thing we've learned from the COVID-19 pandemic, it is that we can't predict the future. However, we *can* plan for potential impacts to our school communities. One of the most effective ways to do so is to engage in scenario planning. Trends, like those gathered in this book, are a critical part of scenario planning.

Scenario planning is a tool to imagine alternative futures; it offers an opportunity to develop stories about how current events and trends may play out over time. These scenarios provide a range of possibilities, allowing a school to prepare for a range of impacts that incorporate both the expected and the unexpected.

> **STEPS OF SCENARIO PLANNING**
> 1. Consider key trends.
> 2. Identify key uncertainties.
> 3. Develop scenarios.
> 4. Imagine implications.
> 5. Develop strategies.

Although scenario planning can take different forms at different schools, there are a few universal components. Generally, a leadership team begins by identifying a focal issue or question to investigate—the issue that would have the greatest impact on the school's ability to thrive and carry out its mission. This step can make scenario planning more manageable and, ultimately, more meaningful.

For example, members of one school's leadership team may determine that their focal issue for scenario planning is *enrollment*. In that case, they could conduct research and engage in discussion to consider the trends from this book's chapters on the Demographic Outlook, Enrollment Outlook, and Affordability and Demand Outlook in their own context. Did their school's admission and yield numbers drop, as they did at many schools across the country? How did particular grades and demographic groups fare during the pandemic? What demographic changes are expected locally in the coming years?

The leadership team could also discuss key uncertainties. For example, will new types of post-pandemic schools arise, offering yet another alternative for families, perhaps at a more affordable price point? How could the school begin planning now for this type of competitive uncertainty?

Another school may identify *financial sustainability* as its focal issue for scenario planning; its leadership team could investigate issues and uncertainties building on the trends from the Economic Outlook, Enrollment Outlook, and Philanthropy Outlook chapters.

Many schools have told us at NAIS that their focal issue for the year ahead will be *well-being*. Given the deepening concerns about student and adult mental health after a year of the COVID-19 pandemic *and* the urgency to acknowledge and address issues of racial inequality, many schools are recognizing how foundational well-being is to their ability to educate students. These schools might research their own students' mental health and the degree of learning loss, the extent to which their teachers feel prepared to support students, and so forth. This research could build on the national trends from the Well-Being Outlook and Learning and Teaching Outlook chapters.

Such research informs the next step of scenario planning, when a team develops narratives of different scenarios that could play out. These narratives prompt discussion, allowing the team to imagine how each of those scenarios might impact key aspects of the school's operations, its internal and external stakeholders, and its programs. Finally, the insights gleaned during these discussions can ground and guide the school's strategic decision-making.

While the grounding of scenario planning may have felt particularly necessary during the uncertain times of the pandemic, there are benefits to scenario planning at all times. At NAIS we will continue to develop resources to help schools incorporate scenario planning into their ongoing processes.

Scenario planning can also become a tool in a leader's toolkit. The pandemic took a particularly hard toll on school heads, who were faced with making constant, complex, and polarizing decisions. When I've talked with school leaders recently, some told me that scenario planning gave them a semblance of control and a way to lead productive, future-focused, unified conversations with their boards and leadership teams.

As we move forward, uncertainty will be with us for the foreseeable future. Studying trends and conducting scenario planning can help our schools navigate that successfully. It can also challenge conventional thinking and open our eyes to possibilities that were previously unseen.

Donna Orem is president of NAIS.

MORE NAIS RESOURCES
for
INDEPENDENT SCHOOLS

NAIS BOOKSTORE
nais.org/bookstore

The Trustee Series, with handbooks to train trustees in their most important duties.

Hopes and Fears and *Better Together*, books for improving parent relations.

Fundraising resources, with best practices for schools, boards, and parents.

And many other books written from the unique perspective of independent schools.

NAIS PROFESSIONAL DEVELOPMENT
nais.org/participate

NAIS Annual Conference, the premier professional development and networking event for administrators, trustees, and teachers.

NAIS People of Color Conference (PoCC), the flagship professional and leadership development experience for creating greater equity and inclusion in schools.

The CASE-NAIS Independent Schools Conference, for development and advancement professionals.

Institutes and workshops, intensive training and peer networking on subjects ranging from leadership to diversity.

Webinars, online events that delve into the latest trends and resources for addressing school challenges.

CONNECTION AND SUPPORT YEAR-ROUND

NAIS Connect, an online community where NAIS members post questions and exchange ideas and challenges with peers.
connect.nais.org

Coronavirus (COVID-19) Resources for Independent Schools, a source of surveys, guidance, and shared solutions.
nais.org/covid-19/resources/

NAIS Community Market, a space where NAIS Supporters who are experts in their fields provide solutions to challenges independent schools face.
market.nais.org

Learn more at
www.nais.org